What would Freud do?

What would Freud do?

How the greatest psychotherapists
would solve your everyday problems

Sarah Tomley

FIREFLY BOOKS

A FIREFLY BOOK

Published by Firefly Books Ltd. 2017

Design and layout Copyright © 2017 Octopus Publishing Group
Text Copyright © 2017 Sarah Tomley
Cover art and caricatures on pages 8, 13, 35, 40, 57, 67, 84, 87, 100, 101, 120, 127, 128, 139, 145, 149, 158 and 179 © 2017 Gareth Southwell Illustration
All other illustrations © 2017 Grace Helmer

First printing

Publisher Cataloging-in-Publication Data (U.S.)

A CIP record for this title is available from the Library of Congress

Library and Archives Canada Cataloguing in Publication

Tomley, Sarah, author
        What would Freud do? : how the greatest psychotherapists would solve your everyday problems / Sarah Tomley.
Includes bibliographical references and index.
ISBN 978-1-77085-986-9 (softcover)
        1. Conduct of life--Psychological aspects. 2. Self-actualization (Psychology)--Miscellanea. 3. Psychology--Miscellanea. I. Title.
BF637.C5T66 2017   158.1   C2017-901896-5

Published in the United States by
Firefly Books (U.S.) Inc.
P.O. Box 1338, Ellicott Station
Buffalo, New York 14205

Published in Canada by
Firefly Books Ltd.
50 Staples Avenue, Unit 1
Richmond Hill, Ontario L4B 0A7

Printed and bound in China

First published in Great Britain by Cassell,
a division of Octopus Publishing Group Ltd
Carmelite House
50 Victoria Embankment
London EC4Y 0DZ
Sarah Tomley asserts her moral right to be
identified as the author of this work.

Editorial Director: Trevor Davies
Editor: Pollyanna Poulter
Art Director: Yasia Williams
Designer: Ella McLean
Production Controller: Sarah Kulasek-Boyd

Contents

Introduction   6

Chapter 1: What am I like?   8

I know I shouldn't — but could you pass that last piece of cake? • I like hanging out on my own. Is that weird? • Why do I keep leaving things until the last minute? • Am I a caring person or am I just a "doormat"? • I was only joking! • Why does it always happen to me? • All work and no play makes Sigmund … • If I was more selfish, would I have more fun?

Chapter 2: Why am I acting like this?   40

I keep looking at my phone every few minutes. Why can't I concentrate? • So I'm 50 and fancied a Ferrari. What's wrong with that? • I'm usually so well behaved … what's with the road rage? • Why can't I stop giving my time for free? • Why do I lie when she says, "Does my bum look big in this?" • I'm afraid of flying … what can I do? • Last week I drove my car dangerously fast — what was I thinking? • Why do I keep watching soap operas every night? • Why do I act like such an idiot in front of my partner's parents? • Why do I keep buying the same brand all the time?

Chapter 3: Other people   84

Why can't I find Mr./Mrs. Right? • Why is the new guy acting so friendly toward me? • How do I stop my teenage daughter getting a tattoo? • Why is my partner such a loser? • My partner is great — so why am I thinking of having an affair? • How can I stop people unfriending me on social media? • Why is my boss always so mean? • My family's a nightmare — shall I cut them off? • Is my partner lying to me? • My boss is so cool — she's quick, articulate, organized and even well dressed. Why aren't I like that?

Chapter 4: What's happening?   128

Why do I keep saying embarrassing things? • What's the real appeal of Harry Potter? • I wish I hadn't sold that house • Should I work for love or money? • Why do I always buy the more expensive option? • What's the point?

Chapter 5: How can I improve myself?   158

Why can't I lose weight? • I'm scared of moving on in my career — how can I change this? • How can I think more creatively? • I'm terrified of public speaking • Should I go into Law like my dad wants me to, or join a rock band? • How can I cope better with the tough times?

Bibliography   184

Index   190

Introduction

Psychology is a very young discipline. It began in the late 1800s, when the two "fathers of psychology" came to the fore: Wilhelm Wundt, a German scientist who opened the world's first institute (and laboratory) of psychology, and William James, a philosopher in the United States. Wundt used scientific measurements to study the mind, while James explored it more subjectively. His celebrated book, *The Principles of Psychology* (1890), dived into subject areas that have intrigued psychologists ever since, including consciousness, memory, imagination, reasoning, intention and stream of thought. Was psychology to be an art or a science?

The phenomenon of consciousness proved particularly difficult to address, and then the work of Jean-Martin Charcot, a physician at the Salpêtrière hospital in Paris, complicated it still further. He suggested that some severe physiological symptoms — such as blindness and deafness — can be caused by psychological disturbance. Charcot hypothesized that this was possible because consciousness could be split into separate parts, which, as James noted, "mutually ignore each other." And so the idea of the unconscious was born.

A few years later, in 1885, a young physician named Sigmund Freud arrived in Paris to study with the great Charcot. He was fascinated by the idea of an unconscious area within the human mind, and he came to believe that this inaccessible part of the brain was the real governing source of our thoughts and actions. Freud realized that the "hysterical" symptoms that Charcot was studying not only had a psychological source, but held meaning in some way. He reasoned that if it was possible to reach the unconscious — possibly through its manifestation in dreams, slips of the tongue

and word associations — this meaning could be discerned and the person's symptoms alleviated. This was the beginning of the "talking cure," or psychoanalysis.

A divided discipline

Psychology and psychotherapy (including psychoanalysis) see themselves very differently, and don't always view one other with absolute respect. Psychologists are keen to align themselves with Wundt and declare their work scientific and objective; for the most part they see the work of psychotherapists as unmeasurable, unproven and therefore questionable. The view from the other side is equally skeptical: the psychologists may study brain functioning, say the therapists, but they have lost sight of the person. A mind is more than a brain, and people are not machines, despite the behaviorists' best attempts to portray us as such. They were pointing at psychologists such as B.F. Skinner (see page 44) and John Watson (see page 80), whose work dominated the field (and public awareness) in the 1950s, and who seemed to demonstrate that people could be conditioned to respond to stimuli just as predictably and easily as animals.

Their work was called into question by the cognitive movement that began in the 1950s and came into public awareness through the work of Albert Ellis (see page 107) and Aaron Beck (see page 29), culminating in *Cognitive Behavioral Therapy* (CBT). These psychologists said that between the stimulus and response that the behaviorists studied lies a "mediational process" such as perception, memory or attention. This is the critical difference between us and other animals, they said, and by studying these processes, we could come to understand all our mental processing.

All the while the debate raged, psychoanalysis persevered, insisting that there is a level to the human mind that will never become obvious through the study of cognition or behavior at an explicit level. In the 1990s, new findings in neuroscience began to suggest the same thing: there are parts of the human brain that work ("think") implicitly, beyond conscious awareness, and control much of what we do, assume and expect. Contemporary psychologists such as Daniel Kahneman (see page 52) have studied the brain's unconscious biases at length, while neuroscientists such as Jaak Panksepp (see page 50) have shown the subcortical nature of the seven key human emotions.

Psychotherapists and psychoanalysts continue to be interested in the psyche — that mysterious part of the self whose behavior is revealed through irrational acts (see page 46), and preferences (see page 150) that seem inexplicable even to the person concerned. Far from having one mind, say the therapists, we

have several, as suggested by Eric Berne (see page 59) and Karen Horney (see page 176). We even split other people in two as well, according to Melanie Klein (see page 123). And so much of this depends on our earliest learning (see page 98), which apparently sets in place our default understanding of ourselves, other people, and what the world is like (see page 30).

Forged by experience

This book uses the format of questions and answers to look at how the theories of some of the world's leading psychotherapists, psychoanalysts and psychologists can be applied to everyday problems. In doing so, it provides many different perspectives into the strange world of the human mind, and the brainpower we have in common, as well as the uniqueness of each individual mind. As the psychologist Endel Tulving noted, humans are the only animals that can time travel inside their heads, and this book will invite you to look backward to the past, forward to the future and extremely closely at the present. You might expect resistance to arise to many of the ideas presented here, but as Freud said, "Whoever goes to a dentist with an unbearable toothache may very well find himself thrusting away the dentist's arm when the man makes for his sick tooth with a pair of pincers." It seems that none of us is entirely willing to countenance the many different parts of ourselves, and Freud was no exception. So feel free to pick and choose your truths, and notice what you "instinctively" avoid. We know more than we think, and think more than we know.

What am I like?

Page 10: I know I shouldn't — but could you pass that last piece of cake?

Page 15: I like hanging out on my own. Is that weird?

Page 19: Why do I keep leaving things until the last minute?

Page 23: Am I a caring person or am I just a "doormat"?

Donald Winnicott

Page 27: I was only joking!

Page 30: Why does it always happen to me?

Page 33: All work and no play makes Sigmund ...

Page 37: If I was more selfish, would I have more fun?

Chapter 1

I know I shouldn't — but could you pass that last piece of cake?

Sigmund Freud

This is the kind of slightly guilty thought that Freud describes as lying at the heart of our everyday lives. Desires arise, are judged, there's a quick back-and-forth internal argument, then we decide what to do. Over and over again. And the reason for this, according to Freud, is that the mind develops three conflicting processes: the Id, Ego and Superego, from which there is no escape. And we're not even aware of what they're doing, most of the time. Even as they guide everything we say and do.

Freud's theory of psychoanalysis is a huge theory that covers everything — it doesn't just explain one thing, like why we fear spiders, fall in love, deny our immortality or love burgers; it explains all of them. He set out to describe precisely how the mind is structured and how it works, despite the total absence of scientific tools at hand for the purpose. Interestingly, many neuroscientists today are returning to Freud for an understanding of what they see on their brain-scanning technologies (which he would have loved to play with, being a neurobiologist himself).

However, back in the 1890s, the only useful tool that came into Freud's hands for delving into the mind was *hypnosis*. Freud was working with a doctor named Joseph Breuer, who had discovered that the symptoms of "hysterical" women — such as coughing, choking and limb paralysis — depended upon "impressive but forgotten scenes in their lives." Breuer was assisting women to remember events that had been long buried and, in so doing, helped to cure their hysterical symptoms. Freud was amazed to see that many of the women's physical complaints disappeared completely.

Psychoanalysis is born

Freud took this idea and ran with it, inventing what became known as "the talking cure," or *psychoanalysis*. It takes as its starting point the idea that much of what goes on in our minds is unknown to us. Most of the time we don't know what we are thinking, let alone why we are doing the things we do. Even if we can come up with plausible reasons for picking this partner, this job or

"As a rule, the ego knows nothing of the rejection of the impulse or of the whole conflict"
Anna Freud

this house, we're not really getting to the nub of it, according to Freud. The rational-sounding reasons are all very well, but they're merely the story that the Ego has had to go along with; we're only hearing the end of the conversation.

The eternal conversations in the mind run between three parts: the Id, Ego and Superego. These come into being during childhood, one after the other. The Id, says Freud, is the mind that we're born with. It is a seething, wanting thing — it wants to eat, drink, pee, defecate, keep warm — in short, it wants and wants and the only goal is satisfaction. If it doesn't get it, it lets us know; it's hard to ignore the yells of a crying baby. Freud said that the Id is ruled by the Pleasure Principle — the Id wants pleasure and gratification, and it wants it now.

Many philosophers and psychologists view the ignorant, untamed wanting of the baby as a phase that disappears, but Freud said that it remains always with us. However, as the baby gets older, she begins to realize that she can't have all her desires satisfied — reality gets in the way. This leads to the development of the Ego, which works on the Reality Principle; it comprehends the realities of the external world and works out when and how the needs of the Id may be met, or whether they need to be ignored.

In addition to taking on board the impingements of reality, the Ego also has to pay attention to the third section of the child's mind, the Superego, which develops last. This is the part of the mind that internalizes the "rules" of the world, as handed down to the child, first by parents

and, later, by other parts of society, such as teachers and lawmakers.

The process goes something like this. The Id wants feeding, with something nice — it wants chocolate, say. So you find yourself thinking that you'd really like a chocolate bar. "Are you crazy?" says your Superego. "You're already overweight. None of your jeans fit any more. No one should be this fat! You should be ashamed of yourself!" The Ego is poised between these two screaming creatures, one insisting on what it wants (what you want) and the other criticizing the hell out of you for wanting it. The Superego acts like a conscience, but it is not a wise, philosophical creature; in fact, it is as blindly accepting in its own way as the Id is indiscriminate in its wants — the Superego

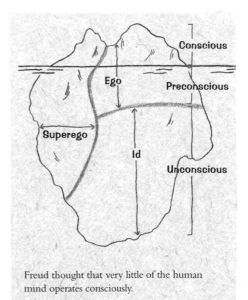

Freud thought that very little of the human mind operates consciously.

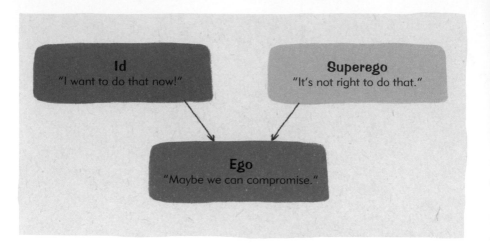

internalizes "rules" given to it by others without first examining them, and these then act as a kind of background programming for the rest of our lives, telling us what we should or shouldn't be doing.

The way that the Superego tries to get us to obey its injunctions is by delivering biting criticism. The Ego tries to fend off its attacks, while also looking out to the external world to see what the reality of the situation is and how to soothe the Id, either by helping it accept a loss or giving it what it wants. So you might take the chocolate, feeling guilty as you eat it because of the grumbling Superego, which may continue to deliver scathing thoughts. Or, alternatively, you might resist the urge (the Ego sides with the Superego) and experience a feeling of superiority (the Superego got its way), along with a faint whiff of disappointment (coming from the Id, which was denied its wish).

Sometimes we're aware of these inner conflicts, but most of the time we're not — this is unconscious processing. Freud says that some of the wishes that come up from the Id are so unacceptable ("I'll have sex with her!" or "I'll kill that man!") that we want to get rid of them immediately — to pretend we never even had such thoughts. This is where we come up with a brilliant set of defense mechanisms, aimed at banishing thoughts from our own minds and hiding them from other people. These operate unconsciously to protect us from experiencing excessive anxiety about our thoughts and impulses, and they happen so fast that we are not even aware of anything having taken place.

"My memory says I did it. My pride says I could not have done that. In the end, my memory yields."
Friedrich Nietzsche

"The ego ... is not even master in its own house, but must content itself with scanty information of what is going on unconsciously in its mind."

Sigmund Freud

Internal/external conflict

Imagine, for instance, that your boss does something so incredibly irritating that you briefly experience an urge to hit him. This is completely unacceptable to you and everyone else, so you need to "get rid of" the impulse in some way. There are several defenses that you might call up to do this. You might pretend to yourself that nothing happened (denial) or that someone else in the office really wants to do it (projection). Or you could shift the desire away from its real target and toward a slightly more acceptable object, such as a chair leg, and kick that instead (displacement). Or you might express feelings that are the complete opposite to your real ones and be more friendly toward him than usual (reaction formation). Many of our defenses were defined by Freud's daughter, Anna, who noted that: "Whether it be dread of the outside world or dread of the Superego, it is the anxiety which sets the defensive process going."

Freud thought that most of the time we manage this external/internal conflict quite well, but sometimes the relentless effort to control our destructive impulses and fend off the criticisms of the Superego proves too much, resulting in anxiety, depression and a myriad of psychological problems (or "neuroses"). He suggested that the only "cure" was to sneak past the defenses somehow and get back to the original wish or desire; to understand the argument taking place among the different parts of the self from the very beginning, with

courage and a complete willingness to accept the unacceptable. This is not easy.

So why psychoanalysis?

Psychoanalysis is a search for the truth that is thought to lie in the darkness just beyond the reach of our conscious, rational minds. Later therapies, such as Cognitive Therapy and Behavioral Therapy, insist that psychological problems can be solved without addressing more than the conscious symptoms, but Freud suggested that "when the wayfarer whistles in the dark, he may be disavowing his timidity, but he does not see any the more clearly for doing so." His suggestions were not scientific, nor were they for the fainthearted, and most of psychology seems hell-bent on finding different explanations for our actions, as shown in this book. Freud, of course, would find the prodigious strength of that effort endlessly fascinating.

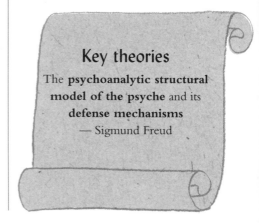

Key theories

The **psychoanalytic structural model of the psyche** and its **defense mechanisms**
— Sigmund Freud

I like hanging out on my own. Is that weird?

Carl Jung • Isabel Briggs Myers • Katharine Briggs

In 1936 the great psychotherapist Carl Jung wrote: "It gradually became clear to me that there must be two fundamentally different general attitudes which would divide human beings into two groups … [which] I have called … extraversion and introversion." These two types have a different focus and way of recharging their batteries: extraverts like to focus on the external world, and get energy from being among other people, while introverts like yourself focus on the internal, subjective world, and recharge by "hanging out on their own."

Since **Jung**'s rather dramatic and swashbuckling slice through the human personality, researchers and theorists have insisted that there are more than two parts involved. Today's MBTI (the **Myers–Briggs** Type Indicator) is a test that divides people into 16 different personality types, with such apparent accuracy that today more than 3.5 million tests are carried out by recruitment firms and hiring companies each year.

However, as the MBTI grew from Jung's original model, it's worth returning to his ideas for a basic understanding. Jung was suggesting that our apparently random behavior makes sense if we see it as guided by two different ways of processing information. Extraverts are more influenced by their surroundings, and introverts more by their own intentions; and the information processed is judged in different ways. Jung gives the example of two people arguing, with one saying, "Now, look here, fellow, these here are the facts; this is reality," while the other begins his reply by saying, "But I think, I hold…" which sounds "like nonsense to the extravert" who insists on the primacy of external fact. What he is missing, Jung says, is that the other person is in touch with a rich inner world — an inner reality that has as much validity as the outer one.

Jung notes that the person who pays more attention to the external world thinks that he "is more valid," because he equates external-world facts with reality, and sees the introvert as a dreamer. However, Jung is keen to stress that the inner world is also powerfully real, with moving images that are similar to those received from the externally perceived world. These inner-world stories are known as *fantasies,* and Jung claims they are as powerful as facts: "When a man has a certain fantasy, another man may lose his life, or a bridge is built … Everything you do here, all this, was fantasy to begin with." Fantasy is not nothing, he claims; it is not a tangible object, but it is nevertheless a fact. So the introvert should not allow himself to feel apologetic for these fantasies, which have been key

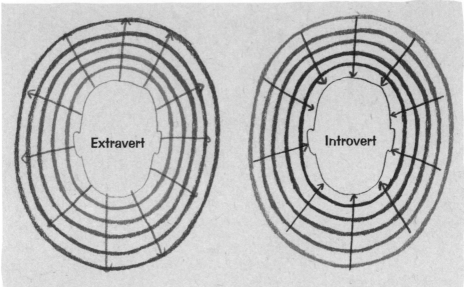

Extraverts focus on the external world and gain their energy from it. Introverts find the inner world of thinking and daydreaming more creative and interesting. They regain energy by spending time alone.

to all the world's inventions and keenest perceptions. The world needs both introverts and extraverts.

Four functions

Along with his two fundamental personality types, Jung suggested that people had strengths and weaknesses in four important functions: thinking, feeling, sensation and intuition. These four were later to become instrumental in the very popular MBTI test. Jung suggested that sensation tells you that there is something; thinking tells you what that is; feeling tells you whether it is pleasant or not (and should be accepted or rejected); and intuition gives you a hunch as to what is happening. Intuition, he said, is hard to explain in ordinary terms. Each of us is stronger or weaker in all these areas to some degree.

In the MBTI, these four factors are played against one another, together with two more. At its most basic level, the test asks if someone prefers to focus on the outer world or inner world (Extraversion vs. Introversion); to focus on basic meaning or on interpreting and adding meaning (Sensing vs. Intuition); to decide by logic and consistency or by people and special circumstances (Thinking vs. Feeling); and to decide quickly or to prefer to remain open to new information (Judging vs. Perceiving). Depending on the levels of preference, the full test then classifies a person as being one among the 16 personality types. An "ISTJ," for instance, is someone whose attitudes are Introversion, Sensing, Thinking and Judging. This personality type is known as "The Inspector," with a wealth of defined

> *"His retreat into himself is not a final renunciation of the world, but a seach for quietude, where alone it is possible for him to make his contribution to the life of the community."*
> Carl Jung

preferences, such as liking detail, upholding rules and gathering facts.

It's not just about being alone

Introverts like to recharge by being alone. Being on their own, somewhere quiet and peaceful, is very important to them (and not "weird" in the least). They benefit from having time to reflect, daydream and think things through. They prefer interesting, intimate, one-to-one conversations to shouting across a crowded bar, and they love to talk about big topics that are really meaningful to them. They make great listeners and writers (J.K. Rowling is a self-professed introvert). Given that extraverts love talking, prefer acting to thinking, and are happiest when doing the most adrenaline-filled activities, it is not surprising that many partnerships (romantic and business) are a successful combination of extravert and introvert.

The neuroscience

Recent neurological studies have shown some interesting differences between the brains of people identifying themselves as introverts and extraverts. Extraverts seem to be hardwired to allocate an unusual amount of their attention toward faces, and in doing so, experience a rush of the "reward" neurotransmitter (a type of brain chemical) called dopamine, which is also implicated in addictive behavior.

In addition, it seems that extraverts use a faster-acting, shorter brain pathway during information processing than introverts, which travels through areas of the brain dealing with sensory processing (sight, sound, taste, touch). This pathway also depends on dopamine. But here's the drawback — extraverts are not very sensitive to dopamine. They need more than introverts for it to work its magic — and one fast way to increase dopamine levels is through raising adrenaline levels, which can be achieved by doing new, fast, exciting and dangerous things — like singing karaoke at a bar, dancing with a stranger or bungee jumping. So by getting out and doing exciting things, especially with other people (faces!), they experience the reward chemical dopamine, enjoy a few immediate, intense zaps of happiness, and everything feels good.

Meanwhile, the introvert is going about things very differently. It seems that introverts have more blood flow to the brain than extraverts, and this travels along a more complicated pathway during information processing, to the parts of the brain involved with internal experiences, such as remembering, planning and solving problems. In addition, they are extremely sensitive to dopamine, so they need very little before feeling overstimulated (in other words, they need to avoid parties!). Their neurotransmitter of choice is a different one — acetylcholine — with a very different effect.

This chemical promotes a feeling of calm alertness and relaxation; it leads to improved memory, easier learning and greater cognitive flexibility. It seems that an introvert's brain is seeking out experiences that lead to a release of a "contentment" chemical in order to function really well, while an extravert's brain is searching for exciting, people-oriented activities that will release the instant "high" of dopamine.

So is there a problem?

All the advice, from Jung to current researchers, is that there isn't a problem unless you were to fight against accepting the kind of person you are and the things you like doing. For instance, if you were an introvert and suddenly determined to party hard, never taking time out, it's likely that you would begin to feel depleted. In the same way, an extravert would feel strangely sapped of energy if he or she stayed at home without seeing anyone all week. Also, you might need to choose your career with care, because it is possible to wind up in a social or workplace culture that expects its members to behave in one particular way, and finding yourself in the wrong one could lead to damage to your health and happiness. Jung has a few words of advice for the introvert: "His own world is a safe harbour, a carefully tended and walled-in garden … His best work is done with his own resources, on his own initiative, and in his own way."

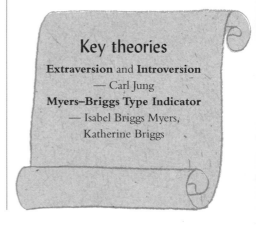

Key theories

Extraversion and **Introversion**
— Carl Jung
Myers–Briggs Type Indicator
— Isabel Briggs Myers,
Katherine Briggs

Why do I keep leaving things until the last minute?

Sigmund Freud • Tim Urban • Dan Ariely • Klaus Wertenbroch

When I was at university, I'd occasionally feel slightly envious watching procrastinators mooching about and having fun while the rest of us were slogging away in the library. Annoyingly, they still managed to hand in their essays come deadline day. So is procrastination a problem?

For all the fun that procrastinators seem to be having, it seems that their internal worlds are not fun at all. Studies into procrastination among college students have shown that although procrastinators initially experience less stress than their peers, over the course of just one term they report higher cumulative amounts of stress and illness, as well as ending up with lower grades.

What's happening?

When a procrastinator is faced with a task — of their own choice or at another's request — they either put off starting it, or if they do begin, they quickly drop it and make themselves scarce. For instance, you might sit down to write an essay but then decide that you'll just look at Facebook for five minutes before starting, only to find that three hours have gone by and there's "no point starting now." Or the goal might be much larger, such as deciding to get physically fit, but then realizing that "my sneakers are too worn out — I'll need to get new ones before I can go running."

Freud would identify these kinds of self-comments as *defenses*, which in simple terms are strategies we use to shift our thoughts (and bodies) away from something that causes us to experience a sort of "flinching" inside — an internal "Ow!" If that happens, one of our defenses will step in automatically and unconsciously in an effort to make us feel better. Faced with the unpleasant task of writing an essay, for instance, procrastinators often (unconsciously) use the defense of Denial, which is a way of blocking our awareness of external events. You might tell yourself that there's a whole week to go before it's due, so you don't really need to do anything now. Whoosh! The essay is off your desk. Or you might use Rationalization — a cognitive distortion of the facts that gets us out of a tight spot. Perhaps you tell yourself you're not in the right mood now, or that you need to do much more research before

> "Cut down one tree.
> And if you can't cut a whole tree, cut three branches."
> Joseph R. Ferrari

> *"Nothing is so fatiguing as the eternal hanging on of an unfulfilled goal."*
> William James

starting to write. And with that you turn to the Internet with the intention of researching quarks, only to find yourself watching "classic fails" on YouTube some three hours later.

An internal conflict

Procrastination could be seen as a state of mental paralysis, caused by a conflict between a conscious wish (to get fit or do the essay) and an unconscious wish (to avoid it), and here's the tricky part: by its very nature an unconscious wish is just that — unconscious. We don't know why we keep moving away from the task in hand, even though on some other level, we want to do it. Self-confessed procrastinator and writer **Tim Urban** suggests that this is not quite right; he says that we don't want to do the task — we want to have completed it already, to have it behind us. So it is the doing of it that seems impossible.

If it is a problem of "doing," say the psychologists, it's possible to come up with some answers. Behavioral researchers **Dan Ariely** and **Klaus Wertenbroch** suggest that procrastinators can benefit from "self-binding" by introducing their own deadlines along a critical path. They claim that procrastination is really a problem of self-control, where people choose short-term relief over long-term goals, so it operates in the same way as other decisions involving self-control. For instance, I might decide to go on a diet. But when faced with a delicious chocolate cake on a restaurant menu, I might give in

to temptation. After the meal I might regret having eaten the cake and be racked with guilt and even self-hatred ("I'm a useless person for giving in so easily, what was I thinking? I'll never get thin.").

If it is really just a question of doing something differently and shoring up self-control, psychology abounds with ideas for ways to do this, from setting smaller goals-within-goals, defining and time-limiting each step of the way, rewarding progress and visualizing the future with the task achieved. Professor Katherine Milkman suggests bundling a task you don't want to do with something you do. If you love running, for instance, and have a heavy book you need to plow through for work, download it in audio format and listen to it while running.

Sometimes a rational kind of approach like this works, but often it doesn't. This is because the rational part of us already wants to write the essay — it's the unconscious, irrational, more uncontrollable part of us that seems to be stopping us. Freud suggested that our minds have three components that must work together to allow us to function in our daily lives (see page 11) the Id (the irrational part, driven by impulses), the Ego (the rational part that must negotiate with the Id to work with external reality), and the Superego (the moral, parental-sounding "conscience" of the mind). In Freudian terms, this unconscious drive away from the essay suggests that the Ego is losing a battle with the Id, which seeks pleasure

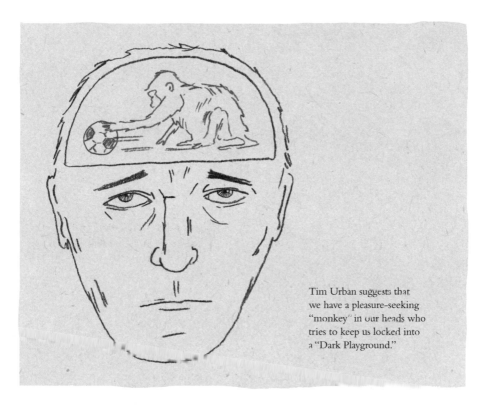

Tim Urban suggests that we have a pleasure-seeking "monkey" in our heads who tries to keep us locked into a "Dark Playground."

and instant gratification. This is the Pleasure Principle — the mind's instinctive drive toward pleasure and away from non-pleasure.

Monkey mind

Procrastinator Tim Urban uses a story to help negotiate the path back to rational behavior. He thinks of his distracting part as a naughty monkey, who lives only in the present and has no memory of the past or care for the future. The monkey voice says, "Hey! It would be OK to surf the Net for a couple of minutes," and with that he leads us into the "Dark Playground," where we do all sorts of leisure-time activities (watch TV, play computer games, go shopping) that fill time and keep us away from the real task.

Even while we're doing this, however, we're filled with guilt, anxiety, self-hatred and dread. Only the "panic monster" that shows up with the deadline makes the monkey run away, allowing us to perform the task just before the deadline.

The key, suggests Urban, is to work with a knowledge of that monkey and its tricks. So the first task is to start, no matter what — and this is the part in which the monkey will put up his fiercest resistance. You'll find yourself working in the Dark Woods (a testing, scary place) while the monkey will be trying desperately to pull you away into the Dark Playground instead, which is an easy, fun place. "Let's go!" urges the monkey. Ignore him and stay in the dark, says Urban, and be

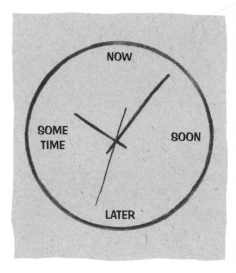

ready for the inevitable bumps that occur when you hit a particularly tricky part of the task — at this point the monkey will be saying, "Let's get out of here!" If you can keep going, Urban assures us, you'll make progress and experience a feeling of accomplishment, which the monkey will enjoy as a "self-esteem banana." This will distract him for some time — hopefully until the last part of the task, when even the monkey can see that it would be easier to head into the blissful playground of "task done" than backward into the Dark Playground.

Isn't that just a story?

Psychologists and psychotherapists have long acknowledged the power of narrative on the human brain, so even if Urban's theory is "just a story," it may be a useful way of helping us to think about procrastination at a "meta level" even as we're engaging in the avoidance of a task. This is the art of *metacognition*, or thinking about thinking, which has been found to be a very effective way of gaining more control over unconscious behaviors. It is one of the most useful benefits of practicing mindfulness.

Like Freud's Id, Urban's monkey is full of appetites, wants and passions, does not take "no" for an answer and lives in constant conflict with the Ego. It seeks pleasure and instant gratification, and doesn't want to know about the constraints of reality. Freud, however, would be most interested in why the monkey is trying so hard to distract you. What are you scared of finding in the Dark Woods? That you are not as intelligent as you want to be? Or as someone else, such as a parent, hopes that you are? Or perhaps you fear life's ultimate deadline? This way to the couch, dear reader ...

Key theories
The **Id** and the **Pleasure Principle** — Sigmund Freud
The **Dark Playground**
—Tim Urban

Am I caring person or am I just a "doormat"?

Virginia Satir • Karen Horney

Who doesn't love a caring person? That's really the question, and if you're asking it, chances are that you've been wondering about that for a very long time. The great family therapist Virginia Satir suggested that, as children, some of us felt we had to find a way to ensure that we were loved and cared for. We noticed that if we were kind and thoughtful, people (especially our parents) responded positively, or at least stopped behaving in frightening ways toward us. Caring promised protection, safety and even love in return. So caring we became.

Satir was interested in the dynamics of families and especially the differences between functional and dysfunctional ones. "Dysfunctional" is a term that gets bandied about in many different senses, so it's worth looking at the particular way Satir uses it. For her, a dysfunctional family is a "closed system," where information and resources are not freely exchanged, but held back from certain members and the outside community. Communication is therefore meager; rules tend to be rigid and maladaptive and operate in favor of one parent or both.

Functional families, on the other hand, are seen as "open systems," where information and resources are freely shared among family members and those outside the family. Communication is free flowing and unrestricted, and any rules that do exist are adaptive and dynamic, responding and changing in response to family members' needs and changes in the family or cultural environment.

Choose your poison

Satir was interested in what it is like to be a member of a dysfunctional family, where communication is reduced to such an extent that either very little is said, or what is said is hurtful, confusing or misleading. The rigid rules are enforced, it seems, by magic, because no one really seems to have explicitly laid them out, but somehow all the family members know what they are. There's a certain amount of guessing going on, especially on the part of children, who need to find a way to fit safely into the family system.

In functional families, where adults focus on the child's needs and don't feel obliged to "lay down the law," a child will never think about whether he or she is loved — the question just doesn't arise. In less functional families, on the other hand, a child learns to recognize which of his actions produces a bad response (the parent gets angry or dismissive, for instance) and which provokes a better response (the parent smiles or rewards

> *"We must not allow other people's limited*
> *perceptions to define us."*
> Virginia Satir

him in some way). In the interests of survival, the child begins to repeat those actions and reactions to people around him that have produced a good response, and so a coping strategy comes into play.

In this way children adapt to their families, becoming the kinds of people who help the family system to stay in balance and operate in a semifunctional way. Satir identified four main coping strategies adopted by children: the Placater, the Blamer, the Super-reasonable and the Distractor. These are not personality types, but communication styles that direct the way we react to other people. Essentially defensive, they don't reflect the true feelings of the child; these are now hidden behind the style in play.

People-pleasing

Satir's Placater has made its way into common jargon as the "people-pleaser" — someone who wants everyone to be happy and will go out of their way to make this happen. The people-pleaser is friendly, helpful, supportive and incredibly generous in every way, giving and then giving more, often beyond what might reasonably be expected. The problem lies in the cost of this extreme generosity; in looking after other people's needs to this extreme, they neglect their own. In fact, they may no longer really know what their needs are, because they've been neglecting them for so long. Having lost faith in their natural ability to be loved, they have abandoned themselves and most of their self-esteem. This is the cost of conditional, rather than unconditional love.

If people-pleasers focus on other people and help them achieve their dreams, it is because they have lost connection with their own sense of self and want to avoid conflict at all cost. Satir's term, the "Placater," reveals what's really going on here: the point of this coping strategy is not to please so much as to placate — to soothe the frayed nerves of other people and fend off aggression by being agreeable, never asking for anything in return and always apologizing, even when they are not to blame. The Placater always says "yes" and never a dangerous "no."

Blaming, computing and distracting

The Placater works in tandem with the Blamer, who places the blame for everything on everyone else and finds the Placater conveniently ready to accept an accusation. Neither of these stances makes the person feel genuinely good, but they do bring about some temporary relief: the Placater feels better when the other person feels happier, and the Blamer feels powerful when others obey him or her and take the blame.

Someone who has adopted the Super-reasonable strategy will appear fair minded and logical. In reality these people are very emotionally detached, insisting that everyone obey the rules (this type is also known as the "Computer").

The fourth type, the Distractor, takes on the role of persuading other people to think of anything other than what is actually taking place. This person makes irrational leaps during conversations and laughs everything off.

24

Placater

The Placater says "I am here to do whatever you want to do. Please stay calm and don't get upset."

Blamer

Instead of taking responsibility, the Blamer deflects it by pointing the finger at someone else, saying "You're the problem."

Computer/Super-reasonable

The Computer is highly rational and non-feeling, saying, "I am carefully thinking through all the options in a logical way."

Distractor

The Distractor's job is to deflect everyone's attention away from a problem by using humor and fun.

> *"I think most of our emotional rules have to be broken. Like: 'I should never get angry at somebody I love' … Those rules have to be broken, because they are inhuman rules that can never be lived up to."*
>
> Virginia Satir

Satir suggests that what's happening with all these stances is that the balance between self, other and context has been lost. The Placater has erased "self" from the picture; the Blamer takes no account of the other; the Super-reasonable person has lost sight of self and other, and respects context only; while the Distractor has a flimsy hold on self and other, and has also lost sight of context. It is through bringing back the lost part — self, other or context — that the true, authentic self can begin to feel safe enough to emerge.

Compliance as a defense

Satir's theories owe something to the psychoanalyst **Karen Horney**, perhaps, who had earlier suggested that we have three types of defense available to us: compliance, aggression or withdrawal. The compliant person, she said, has a strong desire to be liked and tries to accomplish this through people-pleasing behaviors, paying special attention to the "shoulds" (see page 177). She classed this a "moving toward" kind of defense or way of easing anxiety. A similar understanding also crops up in the idea of codependency, which arose from Alcoholics Anonymous (AA). Codependents are people who exhibit such selfless, virtuous and excessively loyal behavior that they act as "enablers" to alcoholics, who are only too happy to take advantage of the unquestioning support on offer so that they can continue to drink.

So am I a doormat?

Not every caring person is a doormat; in fact, in my book, no one is a doormat. But if you're wondering if your caring behavior operates sometimes in a way that causes you hurt or feels like a denial of yourself, perhaps you have recently started to notice your own needs more, which is a good thing. Satir would be cheering you on as you continue to think about yourself and your feelings. She would urge you to start noticing when you feel the urge to say, "Yes" when you're thinking, "No," and advise you to press "pause" before answering. Finally, she might give a warning that, when you do start setting limits, other people will accuse you of rocking the boat. So be it. Start rocking.

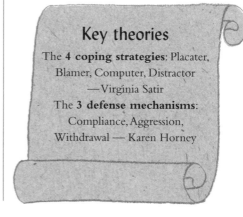

Key theories

The **4 coping strategies**: Placater, Blamer, Computer, Distractor —Virginia Satir

The **3 defense mechanisms**: Compliance, Aggression, Withdrawal — Karen Horney

I was only joking!

Magda Arnold • Richard Lazarus • Theodore Millon • Roger Davis • Aaron Beck

As humans, we're automatically "reading" other people's reactions all the time, and responding in ways that are both appropriate to the situation and satisfying at some level to our own ongoing needs. But sometimes we pick up a mixed message, such as a verbal assurance of words being "a joke" at the same time as non-verbal cues that feel far from jokey. So what's happening here?

Dismissing hurtful words as "just a joke" or "banter" is a classic example of passive aggression, where the desire to hurt is disguised in such a way that the person on the receiving end can't find a justifiable way to complain or retaliate. It's effectively a power play that pretends to be a friendly exchange, and this is the reason that some people in lower status positions find passive aggression such a useful tool. If you come right out and tell your boss that she's an overdemanding, thoughtless tyrant, you may as well empty your desk while you're saying it. But if you ignore some of her emails and turn up late for meetings, you can annoy her endlessly without ever receiving much more than the occasional raised eyebrow

That felt confusing!

Recipients of the passive-aggressive "joke" generally feel confused, which may be explained by *Cognitive Appraisal Theory*, first suggested by the pioneer of *Cognitive Emotion Theory*, **Magda Arnold**. She stated

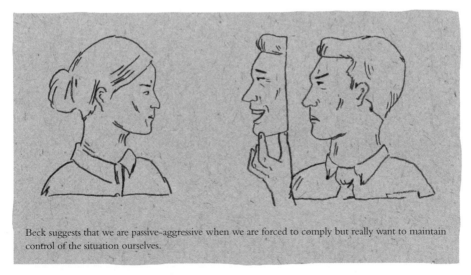

Beck suggests that we are passive-aggressive when we are forced to comply but really want to maintain control of the situation ourselves.

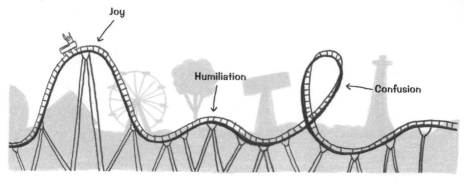

The emotional rollercoaster of experiencing an act of passive aggression.

that when we encounter things in our lives, including people and events, we estimate how beneficial or harmful they are likely to be for us, and this causes a particular emotion to arise in us. **Richard Lazarus** took this a step further, saying that there are two things happening here: we make a cognitive judgment (primary appraisal) about what is happening and what effect this will have on us, and we have an emotional reaction (secondary appraisal), which gives us a different form of reaction, one based on feelings. Although he called these *primary* and *secondary*, either one can happen first, because thoughts and feelings are both sources of information arising from one event.

This makes our judgments of events pretty straightforward — until, that is, you're strolling along a street one day and someone cycles past, shouting as he goes, "Hey! Nice jacket, geek!" Reacting to this, both your primary and secondary appraisal systems are confused — your cognitive system clocks the compliment, but then the way he just labeled you a geek — is that good or bad? So was the "compliment" a compliment or not? You reach for information from your secondary system — your feelings — and they're doing a kind of rollercoaster ride around from

joy to humiliation and back, settling on a general feeling of confusion. The appraisal system failed. Since our feelings and thoughts provide us with information about what to do next, if both of these hit a kind of logjam, we are momentarily unable to decide what to do. We can't take appropriate action, because we don't know what this would be. This may also account for the annoyingly tongue-tied state that's so common to the victim of a fleeting instance of passive aggression.

OK so that's me, but what's up with him?

The term "passive-aggressive" isn't that old, although it's likely that this confusing behavioral style is. The term was first introduced by U.S. psychiatrists who were dealing with uncooperative, hostile and resentful soldiers in the aftermath of World War II. They were said to be acting in a style of passive resistance and grumbling compliance and, if confronted, always had some kind of plausible deniability for their words and actions. Some 50 years later, psychologists **Theodore Millon** and **Roger Davis** suggested a way of understanding what was going on. They suggested that the real problem is that the passive-aggressive person is experiencing profound confusion about himself and others, which is strangely similar to the natural, belligerent behavior of a teenager. This characteristically veers between wanting more autonomy ("Just leave me alone!") and a need for dependence ("Can you drive me to Ben's house?"). A similiar confusion manifests in passive-aggressive people as a very active response to other people's demands, but in a form of action that is focused on resistance. It's like a perfect storm of ambivalence that stops and starts at the same time, and it's perhaps unsurprising that the recipient of the passive-aggressive act feels equally ambivalent when it hits them.

Aaron Beck, the founder of *Cognitive Behavioral Therapy* (CBT), suggested that someone exhibiting passive-aggressive behavior believes that direct assertion is potentially catastrophic. He believes that if he openly disagrees with someone, he risks losing autonomy. This is paradoxical, because it is often only by disagreeing with someone that we maintain autonomy. So he has to disagree, to assert his autonomy, while appearing to agree. Beck said that the two key thoughts here are "No one should control me" and "To conform means I have no control." Taken together, these bind the person into a position of noncompliance while he or she may be operating within a position of enforced compliance.

For instance, imagine you're passive-aggressive and there's a meeting on the schedule today that you want to avoid. As you're thinking about it, the boss passes your desk and says, "Be sure to make that meeting!" The most important thing now has changed from avoiding the meeting to finding a way of defying your boss. So, perhaps you do attend, but arrive late, or without the laptop that you need to work effectively as part of the team.

What if I'm passive-aggressive?

The truth is, most of us act in a passive-aggressive way from time to time, and it's generally in situations where we really want to please people or get their approval, but at the same time we're scared that this feeling means they have some real control over us. This stems from fear, the psychotherapists say, but Freud would likely roar that no, it's rage — rage against an overly controlling figure from your past who insisted you lived according to their rules. Fear stopped the rage, just as outward compliance stops the fear. "Good heavens!" you might exclaim, stepping once more toward the couch.

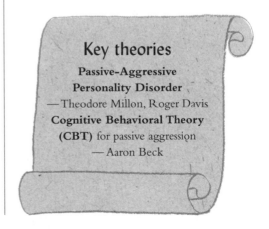

Key theories

Passive-Aggressive Personality Disorder
— Theodore Millon, Roger Davis
Cognitive Behavioral Theory (CBT) for passive aggression
— Aaron Beck

Why does it always happen to me?

Martin Seligman • Antonio Damasio • Emmy van Deurzen

This is the clarion call of pessimists, who send out a heart-wrenching plea as they see all the good stuff raining down on other people. Luckily, the situation is hopeless but not serious, as psychologist Paul Watzlawick says. The world is not in fact tipped against you; it just looks and feels like that. On the other hand, how easy is it "just" to look and feel different?

What is pessimism?

Pessimism is a stance or viewpoint that drains much of the life, color and hope out of the world. In psychological terms, it's a type of negative thinking that stems from some depressing beliefs, starting with "bad stuff happens all the time," progressing to "but much more to me than anyone else" and ending with something along the lines of "it's probably all my fault." In one fell swoop the pessimist has taken a single event in the world, spun it into an "always and forever" thought, and then brought it home to a reflection of himself that tells him that he's useless and there's no point trying.

Pessimists believe that they are unhappy because bad things happen to them, but their negative thinking means that they also expect things to go wrong. In this way, some of their unhappiness depends on their view of the future more than the past.

Pessimist   **Optimist**

30

Turning away from the self

Here's the hopelessness, come to roost — it's not that the world is doing bad things to me, but that I'm a useless person who doesn't deserve good things. From this stems the idea that if something good does ever happen, it must be a fluke — a one-off, never to be repeated (and probably not to be trusted). But as Freud would say, this thought about myself must be kept out of awareness if at all possible, so very quickly the pessimist turns his thoughts away from himself and back toward blaming the world. Which is unpleasant, but on some level, more acceptable.

What about the optimists?

Meanwhile, the optimists are wearing rose-tinted spectacles. They have a positive form of thinking that stems from some powerful beliefs in the goodness of nature — their own, other people's and the world around them. They think that good things happen often, so if one good thing happens, more will surely follow. If a bad thing happens, well, that's unfortunate, but it's only a momentary stumble along the way and probably a good learning opportunity.

Unsurprisingly, optimists have a healthy level of self-esteem and higher confidence than pessimists; they're happier, do better at school, university and in the workplace, show greater persistence, enjoy better health and may even live longer.

Given all that — why would anyone choose to view the world as a pessimist? The thing is, we don't, says **Martin Seligman**, the "father" of positive psychology. We learned this point of view gradually, over years and years of being told things about ourselves and the world at a point when we just absorbed it, along with advertisements telling us which toys to ask for at Christmas. If we grew up in the Western world, where societies tend to be highly individualistic, we will also have been encouraged to constantly judge ourselves, especially in comparison with those around us. Inevitably, many people fall short of the ideal, and mistakenly perceive themselves as failures.

What happened to rationality?

Most of the time we like to think of ourselves as rational people, who simply go by "the facts." However, research by neuroscientists such as **Antonio Damasio** suggests that we're very much guided by emotion. This research has shown that people who have experienced harm, damage or the like in the brain where emotions are generated are completely unable to make decisions, even about something as simple as what to eat. It seems, therefore, that our emotions alert us to where our personal choices lie, and the emotions that arise depend very much on our expectations, which in turn rest on our experience. "What happened last time something like this cropped up? Oh yeah, I messed up." Cue sinking feeling and walking away from the task.

There must be some upsides?

The pessimistic point of view is useful for preventing the rollercoaster highs and lows of the adventuring optimist's life. The only problem is that the level the pessimist is

> *"It is not always easy to know if you are a pessimist,*
> *and ... far more people than realize it are living in this shadow."*
> Martin Seligman

hitting is a kind of flatlining low. It's true that I can manage to avoid feeling crushed if I never ask that good-looking person to go out for a drink, but then I never get to the bar, either. I can feel superior on those occasions when the optimist's dream momentarily crashes, but it won't really shift those rumbling low feelings about myself. Because if I'm a pessimist, I know, deep down, that the problem doesn't lie in a hostile world, but in my useless self.

Learned optimism

Luckily, the pessimist is wrong. There is nothing wrong with him; he just thinks there is. Which means that if he changes a few of his habitual thinking patterns, he can become more optimistic, without having to be reborn as an entirely different person with a different life. If pessimism was learned, says Martin Seligman, then optimism can be learned too. He suggests a system of learning based around noticing your reaction to an adverse event and disputing it. Are the facts really as you see them? Have some assumptions come into play? How many alternative explanations can you come up with for this event? If a friend fails to acknowledge you on the street, does this definitely mean he's trying to avoid you? Or could it be that he was late for work, or thinking desperately of how to win his partner back, or wishing he hadn't played online poker last night? By chipping away at an old habit of negative thinking, some optimism might begin to creep in, bringing with it some color, energy and hope.

The value of pessimism

The diehard pessimist isn't going to buy Seligman's idea of learning optimism for a second, because fundamentally he doesn't want to. Perhaps he wants to be aware of suffering, both his own and other people's. In which case he might be more comfortable sitting among the existentialist psychotherapists, such as **Emmy van Deurzen**. "Embracing life," she says, "means daring to greet the inevitable suffering, anxiety and guilt as an intrinsic part of existence." Suffering is a human achievement for van Deurzen, and the anxiety and guilt that accompany it motivate us to look deeply within ourselves and find what it is that we want to change, in order to become truly authentic. So dig right in — examine the hell out of suffering. Keep going until you stumble upon your reason for being and everything that feels genuinely true, and then come back and tell us about it. Most of our art and literature is depending on you.

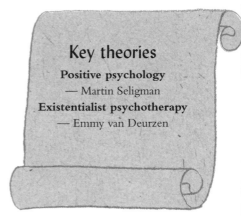

Key theories

Positive psychology
— Martin Seligman
Existentialist psychotherapy
— Emmy van Deurzen

All work and no play makes Sigmund ...

Donald Winnicott • Mihaly Csikszentmihalyi

Adults often don't wish to admit to playing, but the notion of play lies behind all our favorite activities, from computer games and football to mountaineering and playing the stock market. There's something deeply appealing about play that may lie in the fact that it either makes you feel truly present, or helps you disappear entirely.

The psychoanalyst and pediatrician **Donald Winnicott** was fascinated by play. He was aware that Freud thought play and symbolism were expressions of the structure of the mind (Id, Ego, Superego), being projected onto the external world, but that didn't seem quite right to him. As he watched countless infants playing, he came up with the idea that they were creating a third world, between the inner and outer worlds of imagination and reality. Winnicott realized that children use this transitional space as a basis for the discovery of the self. It is where the infant notices herself for the first time.

The background to this idea comes from Winnicott's notion that a baby is at first perfectly merged with the mother, and has no sense of being a separate object. As this one omnipotent being, the baby imagines that she has created everything that she needs or experiences — she feels hungry and a breast or bottle appears. Perfect!

Playing is something that happens in the interface between imagination (the other world) and external reality. It's not quite either one, but gathers content and energy from both.

But then reality begins to intrude. Food sometimes takes a while, diapers are not always promptly changed. As the world impinges, there's a tug-of-war between the baby and reality that no one quite wins. (This is perhaps the first game.) What happens is that the child begins to play, using her imagination to make her own sense of the world and the things in it. As she endows the world with meaning, she is personalizing it and in the process she is creating and asserting herself. Play is what allows us to interact with the world and to continually find out who we are, says Winnicott. So no wonder we like football!

Vital nonsense

Sadly, it turns out that Winnicott was not thinking of football at this point so much as playing with imaginary crocodile families and cooking mud pies. It's precisely because child's play has no rules other than those imposed by the child that it is so enjoyable, he says. Play must not be constrained by the rules or judgments of other people; any attempt to make the child conform, be consistent or "make sense" ruins the whole thing (one senses a toddler tantrum coming on). A collaborating friend or adult is what's needed, to accept the nonsense and reflect back this acceptance of the child's creativity. There you are! How wonderful you are! From this delightful mirror comes a sense of self.

So this is why we like football? Wrong again. Football games are all about winning, and Winnicott says that it's precisely the nonpurposeful state that we enter during play that allows the lovely feeling of dropping all our defenses and relaxing completely. This is the point where we can make completely free associations, unconstrained by fear. It's the point of maximum creativity, without any pressure or thought of goals, and it's the reason that play is so highly prized by some 21st-century corporations such as Facebook (for their staff and on their platform). Play allows us to access the chaos of our unconsciousness and find unlooked-for treasure.

"I know that one way of cooking sausages is to look up the exact directions ... and another way is to take some sausages and somehow to cook sausages for the first time ever. The result may be the same on any one occasion, but it is more pleasant to live with the creative cook, even if sometimes there is a disaster or the taste is funny and one suspects the worst."
Donald Winnicott

" [Play is] the continuous evidence of creativity, which means aliveness."

Donald Winnicott

> *"To understand play is important precisely because it combines in an experiential unity both social constraints and spontaneous behavior."*
> Mihaly Csikszentmihalyi

Poised between anxiety and boredom

Shortly after Winnicott died, the Hungarian psychologist **Mihaly Csikszentmihalyi** (pronounced, according to him, as "chicks sent me high") picked up the ball. In fact, he said, balls and other game devices go back to ancient times, as he found in the many cultures he investigated. He also said that it wasn't so much the finding of self that is important in game playing, as the losing of self, and this has something to do with that nonpurposive state.

Csikszentmihalyi was looking at games with rules (yes, football! Along with more cerebral pastimes like chess, so this applies across the board), and he said: "Play is 'going.' It is what happens after all the decisions are made — when 'let's go' is the last thing one remembers." Play is action within defined rules, he said, rather than without rules, but the rules are agreed by the players. Anxiety is kept at bay by the limits of the game: a die can only turn up on one of six faces; we need never worry that it might turn up a seven, a cancer or an unpleasant partner. We can foresee the possibilities of the game and we can find an interesting balance between the chaotic worry associated with many of life's challenges and the boredom of doing nothing. And even if everything goes wrong, who cares? It's only a game, after all.

Losing the self

Where Winnicott feels the self forming in play, Csikszentmihalyi sees it disappearing. When you are playing a game, he says, your unselfconscious attention to your own actions transcends everything else; you lose all sense of yourself as reflected in other people's eyes, and are absorbed in the task at hand. You lose sense of the real world as having any importance: "As a pitcher steps up to the plate, it is useless to ask him for an opinion on the Vietnam War." Your world shrinks to the pitcher's mound or strike zone, and the entire world of social expectations falls away.

Csikszentmihalyi said that this state of being is so intensely pleasurable that it accounts for "the best moments in our lives." He described this state of oneness with one's action as "flow" and suggests that this is one of the keys to human happiness (see page 148). So that's why we like football. Possibly.

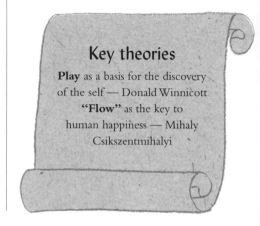

Key theories

Play as a basis for the discovery of the self — Donald Winnicott
"Flow" as the key to human happiness — Mihaly Csikszentmihalyi

If I was more selfish, would I have more fun?

Dorothy Rowe • Melvin Lerner

This question throws up a further question, about what it means "to be selfish." If you assume that, at the most basic level, it means "I'm going to do what I want, and I don't care about you," it produces in many of us a kind of shudder. It feels rude, uncaring, "not nice." But where does this sense come from? And why does "doing what I want" seem to carry with it that second assumption, that "I don't care about you"?

Psychologists and psychotherapists seem to be coming to a basic agreement of some sort about the origin of these rules. Children must be socialized into their culture, so they "fit" and prosper, rather than being seen as oddballs or misfits with little chance of thriving. The responsibility for this socialization lands first on parents, who find it is their duty to teach their child about "how the world works" and what they must do in order to have a good life.

The psychologist **Dorothy Rowe** took a long, hard look at the word "good" in that context. It seems somehow a given that children should learn to be good, and yet the definition of what that is, exactly, depends on the person handing out the rules. Suppose that one parent has very strong religious views, for instance, or comes from a family that viewed pleasure as somehow sinful — how would this affect the rules they consciously or unconsciously draw up for their family? Even in less strict families there may be rules about selfishness dressed as manners, such as "Never take the last cookie" or "Those who ask don't get."

Quick learners

A young child quickly grasps the family rules and the consequences of breaking them. This may look to the outside world like a simple verbal reprimand, but it gains power by being internalized by the child along with an accompanying feeling of guilt. Where these reprimands are repeatedly issued, even in the most trivial of circumstances, a child begins to feel that she can't measure up — the standards seem unreachable and she feels that she will continually fail.

At the same time, there's some interesting myth-making going on. When we're born, we cannot make any sense of the colors, light and sounds that surround us, but gradually we begin to make meaning of it all. We're

"To be happy, we must not be too concerned with others."
Albert Camus

> *"Let go of that childish belief, accept randomness, tolerate chaos, and the whole thing slides into place."*
> Tim Lott

helped along by parents and teachers, and also by stories, gained from books, TV, the cinema, theater and most forms of culture, both high and low. These narratives generally come down to one main theme: the good guys will win and the bad guys will be defeated and punished. Sometimes this may be unclear — as, for example, when we seem to be willing the "bad guys" on to victory (like the bank-robbing Butch Cassidy and Sundance Kid), but this only tends to occur where they have been clearly identified as "the good guys" in reality.

This narrative plot says two things: first, that the world is a just, orderly and predictable place; and second, that if a person is good, then good things will happen to her. Unfortunately, these ideas not only become firmly entrenched in our beliefs, they also play havoc with our sense of self when bad things happen. If good people receive rewards (the good guys win), and I'm experiencing a life event that feels like some kind of punishment, then I can't be a good person. I must be a bad person.

Only the good get depressed

Rowe insists that this belief is fundamental to depression. People who have chosen to be "bad" and to rebel deliberately are on solid ground and quite happy, even though they might be said to be acting selfishly by living the way *they* want to live and by their own rules. In contrast, those who are trying to be "good" and then fall foul of the rules

(other people's rules) see themselves as having failed — they conclude that they just weren't good enough. If those are the rules, everyone else must be doing OK with them. Even as adults, when "good people" (those trying to be good) suffer loss or trauma, they feel that on some level they must have deserved it, because bad things only happen to bad people. This is their punishment, because they have failed to measure up. It is the trying so hard to be good that leaves them feeling inadequate, according to Rowe, who concludes that "only good people get depressed."

The underlying belief in the world as a just and predictable place backs up our mistaken belief that good people are rewarded and serves to heighten the sense of inadequacy. If we believe that the world is predictable and runs along scientific lines like cause and effect, then there is "obviously" a cause or reason for everything. So there must be a reason behind the hardest of life's challenges. While searching for a reason ("Why me?") for being hurt in a car accident, for instance, a person who believes that the world is just comes to one inevitable conclusion: I must have deserved this.

Make the world fit the myth

The psychologist **Melvin Lerner** looked into our belief in the "just world" and found that we will defend this idea against pretty much all evidence to the contrary. In fact, we will change the facts to fit this story. In a classic experiment with psychologist Carolyn

If we've been told often not to take the last cookie, it may seem a devilish act!

Simmons in 1966, people were shown live images of a woman apparently receiving agonizing electric shocks for failing to answer questions correctly. When they were given the option to end the shocks, they did so, but when they were told there was nothing they could do to intervene and they would have to helplessly sit and watch, they began to change their opinion of the woman being hurt. She must deserve it, in some way, they said; she wasn't really an innocent victim. She couldn't be (it's a just world). There had to be a fit between her fate and her character — if they couldn't change her fate, they would change her character.

We all like to think that we'd act differently, but research seems to disprove this. We need to believe that the world is just and predictable, and that it follows an orderly set of laws, because otherwise we're living in a chaotic, nightmarish world where anything could happen. Which is, of course, true. But it's an unbearable truth. So we use a hefty dose of denial (thank you, Freud) and will sacrifice even our own sense of worth to keep intact the myth that the world is a safe and knowable place.

Maybe it's time to embrace uncertainty?

Perhaps that's why the rebels — the "bad guys" — are having more fun. They've seen through the myths and are making their own way in a world that's random, chaotic but nonetheless fun. If we can let go of our need for certainty, throw out the rules and see what's actually happening, instead of making events fit our impoverished stack of possible narratives, we could be surprised. There is no answer to the question, "Why me?" Random events happen all the time. So break the rules. Take the last cookie. See what happens.

Key theories
Only the **good get depressed**
— Dorothy Rowe
Belief in a **just world**
— Melvin Lerner

Why am I acting like this?

Page 42: I keep looking at my phone every few minutes. Why can't I concentrate?

Page 46: So I'm 50 and wanted a Ferrari. What's wrong with that?

Page 50: I'm usually so well behaved ... what's with the road rage?

Page 54: Why can't I stop giving my time for free?

Page 59: Why do I lie when she says, "Does my bum look big in this?"

Page 63: I'm afraid of flying ... what can I do?

Page 68: Last week I drove my car dangerously fast — what was I thinking?

Page 72: Why do I keep watching soap operas every night?

Page 76: Why do I act like such an idiot in front of my partner's parents?

Page 80: Why do I keep buying the same brand all the time?

Aaron
Bell

Chapter 2

I keep looking at my phone every few minutes. Why can't I concentrate?

Donald Broadbent • Colin Cherry • Anne Treisman • B.F. Skinner • Hermann von Helmholtz

In the 21st century we are bombarded with information, and our ability to selectively pay attention to some things more than others is a critical skill. If you and I were truly rational creatures, our attention would zone in on streams of information that are most useful to the task in hand, but for some reason — no matter what the task in hand — we keep looking at our phones. What's making them so irresistible?

Everyone knows what attention is and, at the same time, no one really does. Broadly speaking, it allows us to focus on one particular stimulus (the attractive person at the bar) rather than all the others (the many other people in the bar, the bar itself, the music playing, or the drink in your hand). It's a process that involves selectivity, but psychologists are still researching quite how this works. Do we think about what something means and then pay attention to it, or does something get our attention by virtue of its signal strength (such as a loud noise) and then get passed to our cognitive processing areas for meaning?

Back in the 1950s, psychologists such as **Donald Broadbent** and **Colin Cherry** argued about this chicken and egg situation, with Broadbent saying that the physical characteristics stand at the beginning of our mind's filtering system, while Cherry insisted that meaning takes priority. He pointed out that we always hear our name being called, even among a cacophony of voices, and named this (rather delightfully) the "Cocktail Party Effect."

In a move that Freud would admire, **Anne Treisman** suggested that all the incoming information from our senses is allowed through the brain's processing system, but it is weakened so that it can pass through the system at an unconscious level. From this "unattended stream" certain things (such as your name) may grab the attention.

Recent studies, which involve few cocktails but plenty of brain imagery, suggest that attention is a dynamic, competitive system. During information processing, our attention — at any given moment — enhances some information (the "winner") while inhibiting the rest (the "losers"). The process involves many parts of the brain and depends upon two things: your goal (looking for your friend who's wearing a red dress — so all other colors are ignored) and the strength of the incoming stimuli (such as the smashing of glass, which grabs your attention over all else).

Our goals are dependent on "top down" or cognitive processing, so if you're thirsty, you'll notice that bottle of water on my desk as you walk toward me. This means of selection is

The Cocktail Party Effect

endogenous, because it arises within you. If you walk into a waste bin on your way through the office and hurt your shin, your attention will be grabbed by "bottom down" sensory processing from the environment. This is an external or *exogenous* process.

The system has some inherent flaws, because the sheer selectivity of the process means that we miss things, especially if we are placed in a situation that is crowded either in space or time (when information is delivered in a rapid stream). We can also fall prey to "change blindness," which means that we don't notice change elements that are outside our central interest. If you're watching Julia Roberts and Richard Gere having breakfast in *Pretty Woman*, for instance, you may not notice that her croissant mysteriously turns into a pancake. So we miss things in geographical space, and we also miss things in time. And we have experience of this, so we know these "misses" are possible.

The problem with phones may be the way that they bring all this attention-grabbing stuff together in one handy package, and add in few addictive brain chemicals for fun.

> *"Any man who can drive safely while kissing a pretty girl is simply not giving the kiss the attention it deserves."*
> Anonymous

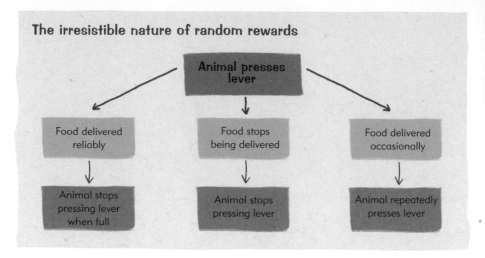

The irresistible nature of random rewards

Animal presses lever

Food delivered reliably	Food stops being delivered	Food delivered occasionally
Animal stops pressing lever when full	Animal stops pressing lever	Animal repeatedly presses lever

On the exogenous level, they have all those little noises that say, "You've got a text!" Or, "Here's a video of us partying last night!" Those external stimuli are pretty compelling. On top of that, you may have some serious endogenous goals — has she texted me? Has that job offer come in yet? Did anyone like my photo? Has anyone replied to my snapchat? Also, given our awareness of missing things while our attention is elsewhere, did one of those things happen and I missed it?

Let's say you get the text or a photo. This activates the novelty centers of the brain and you experience a "reward" in the form of endogenous opioids, bringing an instantly blissful effect that also makes it much harder to drum up the focus necessary for the business meeting you're actually attending (in body, at least). If you respond to the message/ photo/video of funny fails, you get another dose of dopamine, the main reward chemical, for that small "accomplishment," and perhaps some more when you think how great it is to feel socially connected to other people. (Kerching! Kerching!)

Phones also deliver a random reward, rather than a guaranteed one. And the "father" of behavioral science, **B.F. Skinner**, demonstrated that nothing is as irresistible as a random reward (he called it a "variable ratio schedule"). He placed animals in a box with a lever that could be pressed. At first, each time the animals did so, food appeared, and the animals stopped pressing the lever when they were full. When food stopped being delivered over a long period they stopped pressing the lever. But when food appeared only occasionally with the pressing of the lever, the animals continued to press the lever

> *"There is a limit to the amount of information which a listener can absorb in a certain time, that is, he has a limited capacity."*
> Donald Broadbent

> *"In some ways we create our experience rather than its being determined directly by a camera-like process. Perception is more like a controlled hallucination than like an automatic registration of stimuli."*
> Anne Treisman

repeatedly. (Is there a text? Yes! Is there a text? No. Is there a text? Is there?)

Intriguingly, phones may even draw upon the power of "covert attention," described in 1894 by **Hermann von Helmholtz**. He demonstrated that, although the eyes may be directed to one particular spot (the notepad in front of you), visual attention can be directly elsewhere "covertly" — that's to say, without moving the eyes. By keeping a phone just in the realm of peripheral vision, while absolutely not looking at it, we can actually keep a watch on this box of delights at all times.

Is there a problem?

Sadly, yes. Several, in fact. First, there's the way that we delude ourselves that we can effectively multitask. We humans have a limited amount of attention and, if we divide this "pool" among two or more tasks, it either becomes very finely spread (so we're not noticing much about any of them), or one task takes most of the attention and the others suffer. Professor Glenn Wilson found that multitasking, such as trying to concentrate while knowing there's an email waiting to be read, results in greater cognitive loss than someone would suffer from smoking cannabis.

In addition, dopamine acts on a part of the brain called the *nucleus accumbens*. Scientists have carried out experiments on rats that involved offering the rats a lever that, when pressed, delivered an electrical signal directly to their *nucleus accumbens*, imitating the effect of dopamine. The rats loved it so much that they constantly pressed the lever; they did not bother to eat, sleep or have sex. They just kept on pressing the lever until they died.

In 2016 the government of New South Wales, Australia, announced they were going to trial ground-level traffic lights to capture the attention of pedestrians who sometimes inadvertently walk onto busy roads. These people miss all the attentional cues of cars whirring past, car engine noises, horn dips, and dipping pavement edges beneath their feet. The cars, vans, trucks and motorbikes can't compete with the pull of the phone, and attention becomes dangerously lost.

Key theories
Attention processes — Donald Broadbent and Colin Cherry
Random rewards — B.F. Skinner
Covert attention — Hermann von Helmholtz

So I'm 50 and wanted a Ferrari. What's wrong with that?

Elliott Jaques • Erik Erikson • Carl Jung • Irving Yalom

The term "midlife crisis" first appeared in a 1965 article by psychoanalyst Elliott Jaques entitled "Death and the Midlife Crisis." Psychologist Daniel Levinson then carried out informal interviews with 40 professional men and confirmed that he had also identified a difficult midlife transition. The term "midlife crisis" was quickly popularized and passed into everyday language, despite the fact that no research since Levinson's small study has found convincing evidence of its existence. And yet you appear to be worried. Is there a problem?

The psychoanalyst **Elliott Jaques** noticed that a striking number of people who were considered geniuses — such as Mozart, Gauguin and Chopin — had died between the ages of 35 and 39, and he wondered if there was something significant about this time of life. His research suggested that in the case of geniuses the mid-to-late-30s stage is significant, but people fall into three distinct groups. In the first, genius burns brightly from the start, with artists producing miraculous works before dying (literally or metaphorically) around the age of 35. A second group did not even begin to produce great work until they were past 35, while a third group started well then shifted into a superlative gear at this point in their lives.

As a psychoanalyst, Jaques found this turning point was also recognized by his non-genius clients who, aged 35–40, seemed suddenly to become aware of their lives being circumscribed — of having a limit. It was as though the endpoint of their lives had suddenly come into view, giving them a real sense of "time left" in their lives, and what might or might not still be achievable. As youths they had felt immortal, and their dreams had led them to the position in which they now found themselves, but a sudden awareness of death had brought those dreams back into sharp focus. What had they once wished for? What had they achieved? With the end in sight, albeit probably still some way off, would it be possible to do

> "Pause as you stare into the photograph of the younger you. Let the poignant moment sweep over you and linger a bit; taste the sweetness of it as well as the bitterness."
>
> Irving Yalom

everything they still wanted to do? Or was this "it"? Would they be stuck in this job, this marriage and this environment for the rest of their lives?

According to psychologist Joseph Nuttin, time perspective is critical to our motivation. When we see the future as open-ended, we give ourselves goals that involve gaining information and resources. But when we view the future as time-limited, we set goals that help us come to terms with ourselves and our emotions — to deal with what we have, in a more accepting way. The focus moves away from trying to achieve more and toward accepting what we have and who we are. This shift may stem from a realization that death is now on the horizon, even if still distant, but it also acts to focus our attention on learning how to greet this — the hardest of life's challenges — with equanimity.

This is great in theory, but hard in practice. We may not feel equal to the task, and may choose instead to deny death's distant presence by insisting that we are as full of life as ever, able to do everything a teenager might do. Look! I can climb mountains, run marathons and party all night. I'm fine! Fit as a fiddle! I'll prove to you (and myself) just how young I am in heart and mind by buying a sports car, dating a younger woman and getting myself a new head of hair. Trapped and scared? Who, me?

Do women have midlife crises?

There seems to be a general consensus that this sudden measurement of achievement and fear of time running out affects men more

than women. L.M. Tamir has suggested that women are more self-reflective by nature and have been wondering about what they're doing and where they're going all their lives, adjusting their goals and sense of self along the way. Other psychologists have suggested, however, that while men gauge their achievements in terms of status and money, women seek validity through relationships, and tend to judge themselves by how they have been as a mother, partner or a friend. They may also take stock at the midlife point and feel a crisis of identity around relationships, especially if they have devoted themselves to caring for children or parents who no longer need their help.

The psychologist **Erik Erikson** would argue that everyone goes through certain developmental stages during their lives, men and women alike, and the midlife stage poses particular challenges that must be successfully negotiated, just as all the earlier stages were. His seventh stage, termed Middle Adulthood, is said to occur at 40–65 years of age and involves a choice between Generativity and Stagnation. "Generativity" is a state of being that sees as its focus the greater good and the well-being of future generations. All our accomplishments at this stage, he says,

Erik Erikson's eight stages of psychosocial development

1. Hope	**2. Will**	**3. Purpose**	**4. Competency**
Trust vs. Mistrust	Autonomy vs. Shame	Initiative vs. Guilt	Industry vs. Inferiority
Infancy (0 to 1½)	Early childhood	Play age (3 to 5)	School age (5 to 12)
	(1½ to 3)		

should be aimed at helping to make the world a better place, rather than at simply lining our own pockets or seeking hedonistic pleasures. We can use the challenges of this stage — career turns, relationship changes, physical signs of aging — to find new meaning and purpose. If a person fails to negotiate this stage successfully, he may sink into a state of self-absorbed Stagnation.

Might he then buy a sports car? Perhaps. Especially if he has a little of the *Puer Aeternus*, or Eternal Boy in him. This is a term used by **Carl Jung** for men in their 40s or 50s who act as though they are teenagers, believing themselves to be "forever young," like Peter Pan. The *puer* seeks ecstasy, often at the expense of everything else. He prizes new experiences, new loves, new challenges — he will not be pinned down. He has to be on the move, always; if a task or job requires elements of boring routine (and what task does not?) he rejects it and he seeks new pastures, playgrounds and pursuits.

This quest for constant euphoria is a flight from its opposite, say the psychoanalysts, the dark and sinister moods of depression, physical breakdown, and (in a nod to Erikson) stagnation. The midlife point threatens to reveal life in all its truth and ugliness; the body begins to fail, a lack of

"A person does best at this time to put aside thoughts of death and balance its certainty with the only happiness that is lasting: to increase … the goodwill and higher order in your sector of the world."
Erik Erikson

5. Fidelity	**6. Love**	**7. Care**	**8. Wisdom**
Ego identity vs. Role confusion Adolescence (12 to 18)	Intimacy vs. Isolation Young adult (18 to 40)	Generativity vs. Stagnation Adulthood (40 to 65)	Ego integrity vs. Despair Maturity (65+)

⸱ ▯▯▯ ▯▯ ▯▯▯ mean continuing financial struggle — and ▯▯▯▯ ▯▯▯ ▯▯▯ ▯▯▯▯▯▯ lonely! The turning point of midlife awareness, identified by Jaques, threatens to hold up a mirror that finally reveals who we have become. For the *Puer Aeternus,* this is a moment such as the one felt by Dorian Gray when confronted with the portrait that has withered with age, while he himself, the subject, has stayed perpetually young.

We see the flash of death on the horizon in the mind's eye and realize that we are not immortal, after all. We can try to blind ourselves with flashy cars, face-lifts and hair dyes while consuming vast quantities of "superfoods" and exercising with a vengeance, but the flash was there nonetheless. Turn and face it, says Jung. Yes, face it, urges Erikson. "I may be able to help you face it," says the existentialist psychotherapist **Irving Yalom**. "It's not easy to live every moment wholly aware

of death. It's like trying to stare the sun in the face: you can stand only so much of it." ▯▯▯ ▯▯▯▯▯▯ hopelessly toward your sports car. "My dear man," ▯▯▯▯▯ ▯▯▯▯ gently, "although the physicality of death destroys us, the idea of death may save us." Confused but grateful, you sink gratefully once more onto the couch.

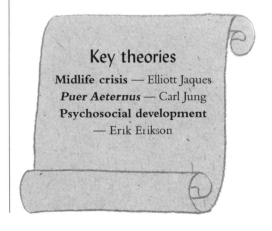

Key theories

Midlife crisis — Elliott Jaques
Puer Aeternus — Carl Jung
Psychosocial development
— Erik Erikson

I'm usually so well behaved ... what's with the road rage?

Jaak Panksepp • Daniel Kahneman

You're driving along a two-lane road, chatting to your partner in the seat beside you, when a car suddenly cuts in front of you, forcing you to slam on the brakes. You and your partner are jolted forward and back; a searing pain courses through your neck from an old injury and the car behind you barely misses slamming into the back of your car. A few minutes later you see the offending car pull into a restaurant. What do you do?

We'd probably all like to answer like the rational creatures we believe ourselves to be: "I might pull in for a couple of minutes to calm down, then pull out onto the road again and continue my journey."

Unfortunately, as psychologists have proved time and again, we're less evolved than we think and occasionally react in ways that reflect the brain functions we share with other mammals rather than the higher cognitive powers available to the human brain. The courts are littered with cases of men and women described by friends and loved ones as "always so sweet and gentle!" who have leaped on other drivers with unbounded aggression.

Did he or she seem like the kind of person to flip off a driver, carry a knife to slash a tire, spit in the face of another person during an argument or punch a man twice, their lawyer might ask? Absolutely not, say loved ones. But somehow these offenses can be laid at their door. So what's happening?

Road rage seems to invoke a kind of aggression that flares up instantly and uncontrollably, even in normally pacific people. So whereas "ordinary" aggression might be explained in terms of personality, childhood experiences, environmental influences or even *epigenetics* (a combination of nature and nurture), something else seems to be at play here. Research by psychologist **Jaak Panksepp** suggests that we need to look for an answer deep within the human brain — so deep, in fact, that we access the subcortical level, which contains structures and systems that we have in common with other mammals. These are constantly processing the world around us, outside our conscious awareness, providing us with a fundamental understanding of what's safe and what's not — what to move toward or away from. Panksepp describes them as "evolutionarily ancient emotional–affective processes" that cause us to take action before thinking, while our more recently evolved cortico–cognitive capacities (which are to be found in the human neocortex) help us think first and then act.

One of the subcortical systems we have in common with other mammals is a set of brain circuits that control basic, genetically encoded, emotional and behavioral tendencies — in other words, a set of "instincts" that come

50

preloaded in us. Panksepp suggests that we can think of them as being similar to the operating system of a computer, which sits in read-only memory (ROM), while our more complex learning and cognitive systems are more like random-access memory (RAM). The ROM-type brain system underlies the RAM, just as the operating system of a computer holds the key to basic functioning, and it is here, according to Panksepp, that our "emotions, passions and hungers" reside. We like to pretend we're closer to the angels than other animals, he says, so we tend to deny their existence, but they are always powerfully in play.

Panksepp's experiments have exposed seven basic instincts: SEEKING, RAGE, FEAR, LUST, CARE, GRIEF and PLAY (the author capitals to differentiate the systems from the normal use of these words). The SEEKING system causes all animals to search their environment for items needed for survival, including both parents and food. No animal needs to learn this, he points out, nor do we need to learn how to experience or express fear, anger, pain, pleasure or joy. Experiments have shown that the seven systems can be triggered by direct electrical stimulation to particular parts of the brain. When this is the RAGE system, animals exhibit piloerection (raised hairs), hissing and growling, and they direct their anger toward anything in the environment that is perceived as a threat.

The RAGE system holds the key to inexplicable and sudden violence, as well as anger as a lower-key expression. Both anger and rage are triggered by events in the

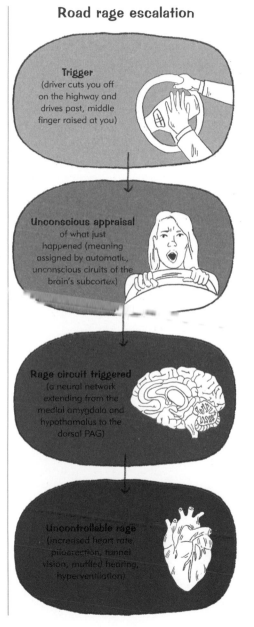

Road rage escalation

Trigger
(driver cuts you off on the highway and drives past, middle finger raised at you)

Unconscious appraisal
of what just happened (meaning assigned by automatic, unconscious circuits of the brain's subcortex)

Rage circuit triggered
(a neural network extending from the medial amygdala and hypothalamus to the dorsal PAG)

Uncontrollable rage
(increased heart rate, piloerection, tunnel vision, muffled hearing, hyperventilation)

> *"Next time you get angry, have a little bell go off in your mind and ask yourself: am I hurting? Am I afraid? Or am I experiencing shame or humiliation? You'll find there's at least one, at all times."*
> Jacques Verduin

environment, but the emotion itself arises because certain types of stimuli access the RAGE circuitry in the brain. Even babies are easily triggered; hold a baby's arms to its sides for just a few seconds and you will see the baby become enraged by this restriction on her freedom of action. This is a key trigger for the RAGE circuit, along with frustration — because freedom of movement and achieving a sought-after goal are part of the SEEKING system. It seems these two systems are closely related: events that thwart the SEEKING system can trigger the RAGE circuitry. As Panksepp says: who hasn't experienced a brief flash of frustration-induced anger when a vending machine takes your money without dispensing the goods? If you're not hungry or now out of coins, you might be able to use the cognitive abilities of your higher brain (the neocortex) to tell yourself that the situation can still be resolved. But if you are hungry, out of coins, incredibly hot and thirsty, and perhaps running late for an important event and *then* the vending machine fails to deliver, the RAGE system is triggered to such an extent that the cognitive, rational system is effectively knocked out of the way.

Fast and slow thinking

This view is paralleled to some extent by **Daniel Kahneman**'s "fast and slow thinking." Kahneman suggests that we have

> ## Thinking: fast and slow
> ## (Daniel Kahneman)
> ### System 1
> Fast, intuitive, unconscious, utterly convincing and full of feeling.
> ### System 2
> Slower, complex, conscious, rational and capable of making judgments and calculations.

access to two different types of thinking: he calls these System 1 and System 2 (see above).

Unfortunately the fast-acting System 1 is "coherence seeking" — it looks for patterns and meanings, and jumps rapidly to conclusions ("He cut me off on purpose!"). System 2 is slower, and can be brought online to question these conclusions. This system is in charge of self-control, but as Kahneman notes, System 2 is often lazy and gets tired easily (in formal terms this is "ego depletion"). In these circumstances, it is only too happy to go along with the (often faulty) conclusions reached by System 1. So yes, that guy did cut in on purpose, it agrees. Self-control is out the window now that you're going along with System 1. What's more, since System 1 does not allow for any ambiguity, not only do you feel like he cut you off, you *know* he cut you off.

52

Triggering RAGE

Panksepp acknowledges the influence of the higher cognitive mind as impacting on the primary-process emotions, just as Kahneman sees System 2 as sometimes influencing System 1. However, Panksepp points out that this is a two-way process: thoughts can modify feelings, but thoughts are also where we carry symbolic ideas, so symbols can modify feelings, too, such as the symbolic gesture of a shaking fist. This means that, for animals, survival threats trigger primary processes but, for humans, symbolic gestures and words can trigger them too. Combine an actual survival threat with a territorial one (a car cuts across your line on a highway) and add in the factor that a loved one is threatened (your partner or child beside you) and an age-old symbolic gesture such as a raised finger, together with internal heightened stress factors such as tiredness, hunger or even a low blood sugar (System 2 needs glucose!) and bang! The RAGE circuit is suddenly triggered at full force.

So what can I do?

Neuroscientist Douglas Fields, an expert on road rage, says the best thing is to learn to recognize the misfire of the trigger — you're not actually in a life-threatening situation and there's no need to "wipe out" the threat, despite the oh-so-convincing feeling that there is. If you feel stresses building up, take actions to lessen them before the trigger is fired. Eat, sleep, take time out, put on some soothing music. If you notice physical signs of anger building (increased heart rate, clenched jaw), use your more sophisticated cognitive system (System 2) to counteract the beliefs streaming from the unconsciously operating System 1. Stop what you're doing. Become conscious. See where you are, right now. For most of us this is not easy, but it can be learned through the practice of mindfulness. In San Quentin Prison, California, they run a specialized insight meditation course that teaches prisoners how to spot the "moment of imminent danger," where anger is about to erupt into rage and violence. The men are all serving life sentences and through undertaking the Guiding Rage Into Power (GRIP) program, they learn how to develop the skills to track and manage the strong impulses that led to their crimes. Founder, Jacques Verduin, says that at the point of imminent danger three things happen: everything speeds up, everything intensifies, then a moment of regret follows. By learning to spot the moment of imminent danger, road rage, like all rage, may be dissolved.

Key theories

The **RAGE circuit**
— Jaak Panksepp
Fast and **slow thinking**
— Daniel Kahneman

Why can't I stop giving my time for free?

Abraham Maslow • Martin Seligman

One of Freud's earliest theories is the Pleasure Principle, which states that every time we are motivated to do something, the motivation springs from an "unpleasant state of tension" that we want to avoid. In other words, we are always motivated to move away from pain (physical pain or emotional tension) toward pleasure. It's not immediately obvious how working for no financial reward might move you away from pain, but Abraham Maslow may have the answer.

Maslow was the founder of humanistic psychology, which was diametrically opposed to Freudian psychoanalysis in many ways, especially in its belief in the fundamental goodness of human beings. Where Freud suggested that we are fundamentally selfish, lustful and aggressive, Maslow insisted that people are essentially good-natured beings who occasionally act badly because of pain. Both humanistic and psychoanalytic approaches agree, then, that we are motivated to move from pain toward

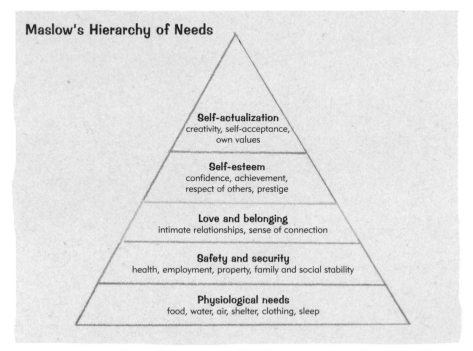

Maslow's Hierarchy of Needs

Self-actualization
creativity, self-acceptance,
own values

Self-esteem
confidence, achievement,
respect of others, prestige

Love and belonging
intimate relationships, sense of connection

Safety and security
health, employment, property, family and social stability

Physiological needs
food, water, air, shelter, clothing, sleep

> *"All people in our society ... have a need or desire for a stable, firmly based, usually high evaluation of themselves."*
> Abraham Maslow

pleasure. Maslow also suggested that the pain involved is often easy to locate, because it comes from an unmet need that might be easily identified.

Maslow is most famous for his Hierarchy of Needs, which suggests that we have five basic types of needs. These are instinctive, or hardwired in our brains, and essential for our survival and health. The hierarchy reflects their priority in our inner ranking, so that the most basic needs — the physiological needs for air, water, food and sleep — must be met before any other kind of need can be considered. The second level of needs – for safety and security – is reflected in our search for physical safety, stability and protection. In other words, once we know that we have the resources needed for breathing, eating and drinking, we'll seek security. Once that level of need is met, our priority (in terms of motivation) becomes love and belonging; we start looking around to friends and family for affection and a sense of belonging.

The fourth level of need is for self-esteem and self-respect, which may be met either internally, through an awareness of our competence, achievements and independence, or externally, through the judgments and respect of other people. Maslow rates the internally gained sense of self-esteem as a "higher form" than the other, not least because it is more dependable than the goodwill and judgments of others, which may be wildly inconsistent.

Why does self-esteem matter?

During the 1930s Maslow attended seminars held by the psychoanalyst Alfred Adler every Friday night at the Gramercy Park Hotel in New York. Adler suggested that a lack of self-esteem could lead to a crippling inferiority complex, and Maslow agreed with him that a low level of self-esteem lies behind most psychological problems. When our sense of respect for ourselves is low, we suffer from feelings of inferiority, weakness and helplessness, Maslow said, and this in turn leads us to a basic feeling of discouragement (and depression) or frantic efforts to overcompensate for these uncomfortable feelings. Unable to generate high enough internal feelings of respect, we focus ever more on gaining the respect of others, most easily by achieving highly, either morally or financially.

We can reach the moral high ground in many ways, and in this way gain respect from other people. One of the easiest ways to do this might be to volunteer — publicly and frequently — for good causes. By this means we might be seen as a "pillar of the community" with all the respect that position entails. This looks for all the world like an easy way to translate action in the physical world into the good opinion of others and a happier inner sense of self, but Maslow would remind us of the dangers in seeking self-esteem from other people's judgments. Not only can they change their minds, but this route to greater self-esteem

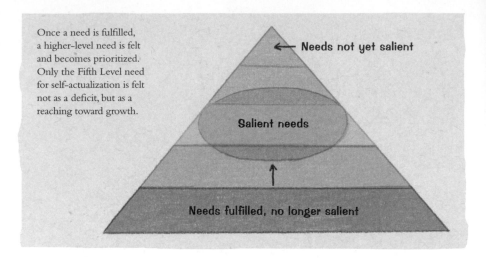

Once a need is fulfilled, a higher-level need is felt and becomes prioritized. Only the Fifth Level need for self-actualization is felt not as a deficit, but as a reaching toward growth.

← **Needs not yet salient**

Salient needs

↑

Needs fulfilled, no longer salient

effectively blocks the way to Level Five on the Hierarchy of Needs: self-actualization. This is a state of true autonomy, where a person's thoughts and actions are shaped not by society, but by their own values. Up to this point, Maslow said, we have been driven by various need deficiences, which we are constantly seeking to fulfil. Once all these needs have been met, we can see clearly who we are, what we really believe in and how we wish to live our lives. This is the true goal of life, where we reach our full potential.

Staring up at all that from Level Four, where we might find ourselves stuck temporarily on the need for greater self-esteem, can feel slightly depressing — not to say daunting. But Maslow's theory is built upon the idea of needs and those needs being met, which means there is always the potential to set the record straight. While he claims that a fixation at a particular level usually relates to an extreme deficit of those needs being met in childhood, there is also the possibility of understanding this and making up for it during adulthood. If you grew up in a war-torn state as a child, you might find yourself obsessing about the need for a well-stocked kitchen or very secure accommodation as an adult. If your parents divorced when you were young, you might find yourself harboring constant suspicions about your partner. If you were regularly humiliated as a child, you might have extreme feelings of low self-worth.

What about affirmations?

Current research suggests that using affirmations isn't the way to go. Tempting though it may be to stick reminder notes featuring positive affirmations onto the bathroom mirror, this is no more reliable than the "mirror" of other people's reflected judgment. It hits only the conscious level (while the deficit sits deeper than that) and can set up an inner argument or conflict ("I am an intelligent person" vs. "No you're not! You're an idiot!") which can be exhausting and create yet another level of tension. The psychologists Senay, Albarracín and Noguchi have found, on the other hand, that asking ourselves questions (rather than making statements to ourselves)

"There are at least five sets of goals, which we may call basic needs. These are briefly physiological, safety, love, esteem, and self-actualization."

Abraham Maslow

> *"The course of [mental] events is invariably set in motion by an unpleasurable tension."*
> Sigmund Freud

can shift self-belief. In one experiment they found that when people prepared for the task of solving anagrams by asking themselves whether they would work on them, rather than telling themselves that they would, results improved dramatically.

Strangely enough, we are constantly telling ourselves what we can and cannot do, as though we don't already know this. Consequently, you might find yourself waiting to give a presentation and deluged by thoughts such as "You're terrible at presentations" and "You're no good at this — you're going to mess up." The interrogative approach suggests catching these and changing them into questions. Am I terrible at presentations? This avoids conflict (or the energy-depleting Freudian defense of denial) and inserts doubt. Then you can start asking other questions, such as what happened last time you gave a presentation? What moments or factors did you enjoy? How do you successfully handle other potentially anxious things, like flying? This method elicits curiosity — one of the few emotions to override fear — and engages your conscious and unconscious mind.

Over the longer term, **Martin Seligman**'s ideas for the three life dimensions may be useful. The founder of *Positive Psychology*, Seligman says that initially we aim to live a Pleasant Life, satisfying needs for health, safety and companionship. From there we tend to move on to the Good Life, which consists in discovering our unique virtues and strengths, and using these to enhance our own lives. This is a good route to enhanced self-esteem, according to Seligman, and is based on a genuine appraisal of our skills and talents, together with a commitment to virtues that are valued in just about every culture: courage, love, justice, temperance, wisdom and spirituality.

Lastly, Seligman says, we find ourselves leaning toward living a Meaningful Life, in which we find fulfillment by putting these strengths to the service of others. So does this mean that constantly volunteering is fine after all? Perhaps. The question seems to be: do you want to volunteer because it is a pleasantly rewarding part of your fulfilled life, or do you *need* to volunteer for some unfathomable reason that feels utterly compelling? "Compulsion" is a favorite word in the Freudian lexicon, and can reliably be expected to lead you once more to the couch.

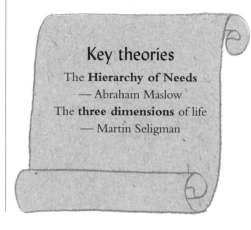

Key theories

The **Hierarchy of Needs**
— Abraham Maslow
The **three dimensions** of life
— Martin Seligman

Why do I lie when she says, "Does my bum look big in this?"

Eric Berne • René Spitz

"Does my bum look big in this?" appears on the surface to be a straightforward question of fact. However, the answer depends upon a subjective viewpoint, because the question is actually asking, "Does it look big *to you?*" This may look like a matter of politeness, inviting a negative response, but Eric Berne would wonder about the real question being asked and about the "game" being played.

Berne was the creator of a branch of therapy known as *Transactional Analysis*, which looks at the dynamics of relationships through our "transactions" with one another, especially in terms of dialogue. He said that transactions tend to proceed in chains (he speaks/she speaks/he speaks ...), so each response is in fact a stimulus — it acts to provoke the next response.

The first rule of communication, according to Berne, is that communications run smoothly as long as transactions are "complementary." This has a special meaning in Berne's methodology, which relates to our "ego state" (or state of mind) and that of the other person. If these states complement one another, all goes well in our transactions. Berne believed that our brains act like video recorders, vividly recording events in a way that captures all the sensory information (sights, sound and so on) together with the

feelings that we experienced during the event. These "recordings" are stored in the brain and, when recalled, pitch us back into not only remembering the event, but feeling exactly as we did then. These recordings cluster into three main groups — Parent, Adult and Child – and they represent three different states of mind that we move between during transactions in our daily lives.

What state are you in?

Berne suggested that the cluster of recordings relating to *external* events experienced during the first five years of life are wired together, and, when evoked, tend to put the person into a Parent state of mind (or ego state). The messages of the Parent state were learned mainly from a parent and might include admonitions such as "Never talk to strangers." In this state of mind, we think, feel and behave like the parental figures

"Family life and married life ... may year after year be based on variations of the same game."
Eric Berne

> *"Games are substitutes for the real living of real intimacy."*
> Eric Berne

(parents and others) from our childhood, and we tend to hand out advice, both to ourselves and to others.

Internal events from early childhood are clustered under the Child ego state, which has recorded emotional learning from significant events, such as "Clowns are really scary" or "Christmas is exciting." When in the Child ego state, we enter the state of being we had as a child; if we had a happy childhood, this is a playful, creative, imaginative state of mind.

The Adult state grows from memories from one year onward, and represents our more scientific self, who notices differences between what is said and what is happening.

This is the state most in touch with here-and-now reality, in a matter-of-fact way. When we're in the Adult state of mind, we acknowledge events as information, and make rational decisions.

What's this got to do with bums?

When Berne said that communication only runs smoothly when transactions are complementary, he meant that both people speaking respond from complementary states. For instance, if Person A says, "Where is my watch?" and Person B says, "On the side table," there is a complementary Adult–Adult transaction. But if Person B responds with

Complementary transactions

These transactions are complementary, so the conversation will run smoothly.

"You always blame me for everything!" he's moved into Child and is directing the response to the first person's Parent (the part who might seem to blame someone). The Adult→Adult question has met with a non-complementary Child→Parent response.

Anyone might ask the "bum" question of anyone else, but for ease of keeping track, let's assume that it's a woman asking her male partner about her bum. If they're both in the Adult state, he could offer her back a genuine assessment of whether the dress or trousers are designed in such a way that they increase visibility of her bum. However, we all hesitate in this situation, because this doesn't sound like the real question being asked. We would all have some sense of there being more at stake, and part of that is that we suspect this is a test of the respondent's feelings about the questioner, not the item of clothing at all. It looks like a question from the Adult state, but perhaps the real, underlying question springs from the Child: "Do you still love me?" or at least, "How do you feel about me right now?" If the man responds in Adult ("I think the stripes may be adding width"), the woman (inhabiting a Child state) might suddenly become angry and say something like "I knew you were sitting there thinking that I'm fat!" The transaction here was not complementary, and communication comes to a standstill.

We all need strokes

In 1800, a child was found in the forest of Aveyron, France, who appeared to have grown up in the wild. Naked, filthy and

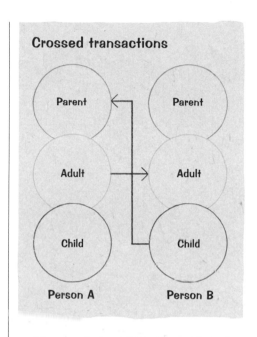

Crossed transactions

unable to speak, the child had been deprived of all "civilizing" transactions, and he was never able to learn to speak or act in socially acceptable ways of behaving. Around 140 years later, research by **René Spitz** into the effects of childhood deprivation on children in orphanages showed that a deficit of personal attention or care by another person would lead to extreme developmental deficits. During the second and third years of life, all the control group of family-raised children could walk and talk, while only two of the 26 orphanage children could do so. Berne suggested that humans have a "recognition hunger," which may be satisfied by words, touch or even slight gestures, such as a wink. Any event that is experienced as personal recognition, he said, feels like a "stroke." Positive strokes such as a hug are better than negative ones, such as a slap, but strokes are what we're after.

Game playing

So is this what's at stake with the bum question? Perhaps the questioner's Child state is seeking a stroke, and woe betide the responder who fails to deliver. Or there may be even more going on here than a simple exchange of strokes. This transaction may be part of a larger game, which is being played out over the entire term of a relationship. In Berne's terminology, games are ritualistic transactions that have a stabilizing function, keeping a relationship locked into a particular form and state of equilibrium, although this "equilibrium" may look painful to outsiders. Games also have a payoff for both players, which may look strangely unpleasant or mystifying to non-players.

Berne described many different forms of games, and was keen to stress that there's nothing fun about them — they can focus on almost anything, from avoiding intimacy to allowing ongoing drug addiction. Moves by the players are highly regulated and both players "win" in some way, by achieving the payoff that they seek.

The "bum" question might be part of a larger game, such as Kiss Off, where one person acts provocatively toward the other (perhaps flaunting their bottom) until the second person is entirely engaged in the seduction. The first person then comprehensively rejects and dismisses the second — the payoff being enjoyment at their discomfort. However, the second

person — let's say he's a man for ease of keeping track — may also be less innocent than he seems, says Berne. He may be playing some variation of Kick Me, which is like wearing a sign saying, "Don't kick me," which inevitably invites a kick, enabling the "player" to keep asking, "Why does this always happen to me?" Or the two players might be locked in a game of Uproar, where players constantly find fault with each other, so they can do a lot of loud arguing and door slamming, while avoiding any sexual intimacy.

So, before answering the bum question, it might be interesting to wonder what state of mind you're in, and what kind of game you're playing. Then consider what may be true for your partner. Or play safe, as most of us do, and simply answer, "You look lovely."

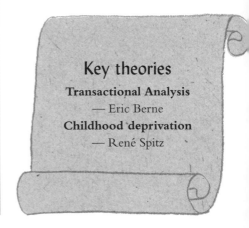

Key theories

Transactional Analysis
— Eric Berne
Childhood deprivation
— René Spitz

I'm afraid of flying ... what can I do?

Daniel Kahneman • Amos Tversky • Aaron Beck

This fear is as old as airplane flight itself. Just 11 years after the Wright Brothers' first flight in 1903, planes were being used for reconnaissance in World War I and reports of "aeroneurosis" began streaming in. A significant number of pilots and crew developed nervous symptoms such as insomnia and digestive problems and became reluctant to fly. Fear and flight had become linked.

It seems those flight personnel had a point. In the 11 years between 1903 and 1914, more than 1,000 people died on flights, and during the war more than 14,000 Allied pilots perished. Aviation was still in its infancy and so there were no specifications for airplanes; this meant that there was a lot less stability (and reliability) in the air. The planes — made from wood and fabric — were difficult to fly, but pilots received only two to three hours' training. They were also completely exposed to the elements. In 1915 the average life expectancy for an Allied pilot was just 11 days, while 9 out of 10 men survived the trenches. This means that, right from the start, flying has been seen as incredibly risky. This was an accurate perception in the 1900s, but that "dangerous" tag has never quite been lost. It seems to be just one of the inaccurate judgments we make about flying and planes.

Real risk or perceived risk?

Fear is associated with perceived risk. It's likely that if you were asked to walk along a 100-foot (30 m) plank firmly planted on a grassy field, you would stroll along it quite easily, admiring the view. However, if that same plank was suspended 65 feet (20 m) in the air, you would probably focus all your attention on the plank and experience a high level of anxiety while trying to walk along it. In fact, you might say, "I'll pass on that, thanks." The difficulty of the task — walking along the plank — is unchanged, but your perception of risk has altered. You might even be unhappy walking along a road-width plank at this height, because you're now filled with thoughts of catastrophe. With increased risk comes anxiety, deservedly so. We experience anxiety for precisely this reason — it helps us to stay alive. But an increase in perceived risk, when the actual risk has not changed, means the feeling of anxiety can be triggered erroneously.

Using shortcuts

Humans are very bad at judging risk, for all sorts of reasons. **Daniel Kahneman** and **Amos Tversky** claim that this is mainly because we use a limited number of "heuristics" or judgmental shortcuts to reduce complicated probability judgments to simpler ones. We like to think and decide quickly, and keep moving. When it comes to judging risk, there are many ways in which built-in biases draw us into faulty judgments. One of these is the "availability bias," which means that we tend to overestimate the occurrence of events that can be called quickly and easily to mind. Events that are covered extensively by the media — such as plane crashes or terrorism — are easily called to mind by association (such as when you are thinking of booking a flight yourself). In addition, if these events create an emotional reaction, such as horror, they gain even more associative strength in our minds and the availability bias means that they now seem "more likely." For this reason, people judge accidental death as much more likely than being killed by a stroke or diabetes, although strokes cause twice as many deaths as accidents, and diabetes causes four times more (when asked in research, people suggested that accidents were 300 times more likely to kill than diabetes).

Faulty thinking

Kahneman and Tversky suggest that we mistake the strength of association (the intensity of the thoughts and feelings evoked by memory) with the frequency of the event. The deadliest plane crash in history happened in 1977, when 583 people were killed in Tenerife when two jumbo jets collided on a runway. That's the horrific kind of news that gets our attention. However, the same number of people die of heart disease in the United States every eight hours. If these deaths were reported on television, we would begin to suspect that a heart attack was just around the corner.

Another way we miscalculate risk is that we fail to pay attention to the base rate. For instance, consider this description of a male university student: he is highly intelligent, but lacking in creativity; he has a love of neat and tidy systems and sci-fi games but feels little sympathy for other people and finds it difficult to interact with them. Is this student more likely to be studying computer science/engineering or humanities/social sciences? If you find yourself opting for the first option, your mind has been hijacked by the "representativeness" heuristic. The student may seem "typical" of a certain subset in your mind, and you may have momentarily ignored the fact that the number of students studying humanities and social sciences is far, far higher. So, regardless of character, the student is more likely to be studying humanities or social sciences than engineering. The base rate — the number of students in certain subjects — is more important statistically than the character of the student when judging probability.

In terms of planes, the number of flights compared to crashes (the "base rate" of crashes) is far lower than for car journeys. Not just slightly, but massively. Research suggests that in the aftermath of 9/11, so many Americans switched from plane journeys to the more dangerous car option that around 1,500 people were killed as a result. The huge shift from planes to cars for the year following 9/11 raised millions of people's risk of injury and death, even as they felt they were changing plans to *decrease* risk. (For the record, the chances of being killed in an airline accident are around 1 in

Types of Thinking Distortions (Aaron Beck)

ALL-OR-NOTHING THINKING: You see things as black or white.

OVERGENERALIZATION: You see a single negative event as an ongoing stream of disasters.

MENTAL FILTER: You pick out a single negative detail and dwell on it obsessively until your whole picture of "reality" is dark and treacherous.

DISQUALIFYING THE POSITIVE: You reject positive facts by saying, "They don't count," for some reason or other.

JUMPING TO CONCLUSIONS: You make an instant, negative interpretation of an event (like an air steward frowning), though there is no evidence to support this.

CATASTROPHIZING: You exaggerate the threat to catastrophe level.

EMOTIONAL REASONING: You assume that your emotions reflect reality, and that if you feel it, it must be true.

"Every one million flying hours statistically results in less than 2.5 accidents."
UK Civil Aviation Authority, 2008

11,000,000; from car accidents the risk is around 1 in 10,000.)

So it's illogical. So what?

Logic may be the best tool we have for defeating fear of flying, or *aviophobia*, as it's now called. *Cognitive Behavior Therapy* (CBT) has shown the most consistent results, and this treatment assumes that fear stems from a thought. The founder of *Cognitive Therapy* (the precursor to CBT), **Aaron Beck**, suggested our problem lies in cognitive distortions that set off a train of reactions. For instance, we make a judgment that something terrible is going to happen ("The plane is going to crash!"), and from this thought, fear arises; we become anxious and as a result we begin to experience the physiological symptoms of anxiety.

One of the problems, says Beck, is that the symptoms cause the symptoms — we have a fearful thought, become anxious, notice ourselves shaking or our hearts racing, which makes us have another fearful thought, which increases anxiety, and so on, until we launch into the full-blown fight/flight response, including tunnel vision, impaired hearing and difficulty breathing. This increases panic still further, until we're convinced that we're going to die. If we start this process with a catastrophic thought — like "The plane is going to crash" or "I'm going to fall off the plank and die" — within seconds we shoot straight to the top of the anxiety ladder. On the other hand, if we can avoid making the judgment in the first place, we prevent the entire cascade.

CBT encourages people to question their thoughts and assumptions, and to open up to the real evidence. Of all the different techniques employed for fear of flying, the two that have been found most useful are "talking back to negative thoughts" (otherwise known as "arguing with yourself") and continuing to fly. Exposure is essential, because this helps normalize the idea of flying through desensitization and gradually lowers your unconscious estimation of its danger. New data enters the system. Several airlines now run courses that offer the full shebang, from in-depth, accurate information (evidence!) to relaxation techniques, virtual flights and finally actual flights with a constant commentary explaining exactly what's happening. One of today's flying "aces" may be just the person to convince you of how much safer flying is today than in its infancy — he or she will have all the information necessary to make a true judgment of risk.

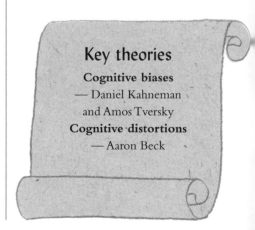

Key theories

Cognitive biases
— Daniel Kahneman
and Amos Tversky
Cognitive distortions
— Aaron Beck

"People have a tendency to catastrophize, to think of the worst possible thing that could happen."

Aaron Beck

Last week I drove my car dangerously fast — what was I thinking?

Marvin Zuckerman • Gerben van Kleef • Daniel Siegel • Sigmund Freud

Dangerously fast driving is viewed by psychologists as falling under the category of "increased risk behavior" and there are several ways that they might seek to explain it, depending on your state of emotional health at the time. Neuroscientists have found answers for explaining the heightened need for risk in teenagers, and have also documented the brain chemistry resulting from adult risk-taking which may offer an explanation. But whatever way you look at it, dangerous driving seems to run counter to all our survival instincts. Freud found this extremely interesting.

A natural high

The simplest explanation for driving seriously fast is that you may have simply enjoyed the rush. People who do extreme sports quickly discover that the reward mechanisms of the human brain are activated when they push themselves to do extreme, death-defying things like bungee jumping. The "reward" comes in the form of dopamine, a neurotransmitter or brain chemical that creates feelings of joy, optimism and increased well-being.

However, there's a big downside to seeking thrills in this way. In 1983 **Marvin Zuckerman** investigated sensation-seeking and found that extreme sportspeople such as skydivers and scuba divers measured high on the sensation-seeking continuum, along with gamblers and drug addicts. This kick-started investigation into sensation-seeking as a negative personality trait, because the people who embodied it seemed to act without regard for physical, social, financial or even legal risk. In addition,

both addicts and sensation-seekers became unable to experience pleasure from everyday experiences such as eating or socializing once their brains were used to being hyperstimulated by the natural "high" of sport-related danger or by drug-induced highs. The flood of dopamine experienced in those situations becomes addictive, so the experiences become more and more frequently sought, while normal life seems to lose most of its attraction.

It's all about power

People with power live in a different world from the rest of us. Vast amounts of money and limitless (paid for) support give powerful people a confidence that often spills over into arrogance. They have less need to follow the rules, because the penalties can generally be avoided, and they may even flout their disregard of rules as a sign of power. Researcher **Gerben van Kleef** wondered whether this worked both ways: if powerful people feel freer to break the rules, does breaking the rules make us feel more powerful?

Van Kleef set up experiments that allowed people to witness and comment upon people breaking rules. They watched as various individuals dropped cigarette ash on the floor, took coffee from another person's cup, or put their feet on the table. The rule breakers were seen as being more powerful and in control than the orderly "rule-abiding" people around them. Examples of rudeness, such as dropping cigarette ash or speaking brusquely, led witnesses to judge the person more likely to be a decision maker or persuade others to listen to him. The researchers concluded that "norm violators are perceived as having the capacity to act as they please." If the speed limit is 60 miles per hour (96 kph) and you're doing 100 miles per hour (160 kph), you may be signaling that you're so powerful that you're above the law.

If the "signaling" part rings a bell with you, it might be worth asking exactly what it is that you want others to know about you. You may want them to think you are powerful, but they may actually think something quite different — that you're a show-off — or in technical terms, a *narcissist*. Narcissists have an inflated sense of self; they not only think that they are special but also that they deserve special treatment. Rules are not for them, either. Narcissists put a

You may see your dangerous driving as a simple "buzz," but Freud would suggest that an internal death drive has temporarily reared up inside you.

lot of time and energy into demonstrating how important and clever they are. They want the best of everything, including food, gadgets and even people, who should be as important as possible. Narcissism can be expensive — financially and socially — when it's a full-time trait, but the odd bit of fast driving might be a temporary narcissistic reaction. Only you would know.

Young and wild

If you're an adolescent, which in terms of the human brain puts you between the ages of 12 and 24, you don't need an excuse. Neuroscientists such as **Daniel Siegel**

"It is this battle of the giants that our nurse-maids try to appease with their lullaby about Heaven."
Sigmund Freud

have found that, along with alterations in physiology, hormones and sexual organs, teenagers have to endure significant architectural changes in the brain. The brain has been found to be capable of change at any age (which is known as "neuroplasticity"), but during the adolescent period, brain changes take place that increase novelty seeking, social engagement, emotional intensity and creative exploration.

Novelty seeking is increased because the brain changes with regard to dopamine, with the result that novelty is experienced as something very rewarding, which increases the motivation to seek out new and slightly

Eros, or the life instinct, is felt as the drive for survival, of an individual and the species.

shocking experiences. At the same time, adolescents develop hyper-rational thinking, which means that the appraisal centers of the brain amplify the importance of the positive aspect of an experience, while de-emphasizing the severity of the negative outcome. Siegel suggests that an adolescent would therefore focus only on the thrilling aspect of driving at 100 miles per hour (60 kph), while minimizing the potential downsides such as crashing or killing themselves or another person.

Bringing death center stage

Researchers have found that some people do dangerous things because they like the extraordinary perspective they gain on life for some time afterward. The experience of fear induced by risk can be similar to that felt by people who have survived a potentially lethal event or circumstance, such as disease, natural disaster, serious accident or other form of trauma. Following these events, some people have reported gaining a clearer sense of their lives, themselves and their objectives, and an enhanced appreciation of everyone and everything in their lives. This is due to an increased awareness of the proximity of death, in direct opposition to the teenage denial of its possibility, though the actual risks involved may be exactly the same.

The death drive

It's not the risk that's important, according to **Freud**. In 1920 he published *Beyond the Pleasure Principle*, in which he said that,

> *"The meaning of the evolution of civilization is no longer obscure to us. It must present the struggle between Eros and Death, between the instinct of life and the instinct of destruction as it works itself out in the human species."*
> Sigmund Freud

although he had been correct in previously suggesting that all mental events stem from a motivation to move from unpleasure toward pleasure, there is something else at work too. He witnessed people returning from war who continued to experience terrifying memories — how or why did that happen? Why did some of his patients exhibit a "compulsion to repeat" frightening or traumatic episodes, either by memory or by reliving experiences (such as rejection) in relationship with him in the room?

Freud decided that there was a second instinct, equal in force to the life instinct, but which preceded it — he referred to this as the death drive. The life instinct, or Eros, actively preserves the life of an individual and the entire species; its drives are toward health, safety, sustenance, procreation and it is associated with positive emotions such as love and cooperation. The death drive — later called Thanatos, after the Ancient Greek personification of death — is the instinct toward death and destruction. It is associated with the negative emotions of fear, hate and anger, along with aggression in all forms. This drive is the most primitive, Freud says, because it is the drive to take us back to the inorganic nothingness from which we emerged. Life comes out of death/nothingness, and is then opposed to it — it must continually resist a return to that state.

The literary theorist Terry Eagleton describes the death instinct as the "true scandal of psychoanalysis" because the idea essentially asserts that all human beings unconsciously desire their own death. The Ego tries to sublimate this desire, or push all of its aggressive drive onto other people (hence the outbreak of wars), but we are instinctively drawn toward a return to our original, inorganic state of nothingness. Hence the pull of the deep water at the end of the pier, the lure of unprotected sex with a stranger, and the urge to put your foot down on the accelerator. Tread lightly, Freud would warn, for you are touching on the most primitive of instincts and it is hell-bent on self-destruction.

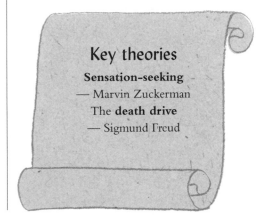

Key theories

Sensation-seeking
— Marvin Zuckerman
The **death drive**
— Sigmund Freud

Why do I keep watching soap operas every night?

Robert Kubey • Mihaly Csikszentmihalyi • Robin Dunbar • Bluma Zeigarnik

You're not alone. TV is the industrialized world's most popular pastime — on average, people spend three hours a day watching TV, which is around half their leisure time. Over the course of a lifetime spanning 75 years, this adds up to nine years spent watching TV. And of all the TV programs on offer, soaps seem to grab us and refuse to let go. It's actually us not letting go of the shows, of course, but it feels strangely as if it's the other way around. In much the same way as the whiskey bottle calls to the alcoholic, perhaps?

There's nothing wrong with watching TV, unless you think there is. People who watch TV for fewer than two hours a day don't spend any time worrying about it, but "heavy users" who watch for four hours a day or more say that they wish they watched less; they watch for longer than they plan to, but feel unable to turn off the TV and walk away. Researchers **Robert Kubey** and **Mihaly Csikszentmihalyi** found that this is true despite the fact that watching TV becomes less rewarding the longer you do it, according to the self-reports of these heavy users.

It's perhaps worth wondering whether Kubey and Csikszentmihalyi were expecting to find addictive behavior, given that they refer to TV viewers as "users," but perhaps this is because they found many similarities between people who watch a lot of TV and substance abusers. For instance, both groups make repeated (unsuccessful) attempts to reduce use, both experience withdrawal when the "drug" is withdrawn, both "use" the drug more often than they intend to, and both groups generally devote a huge amount of time to using the drug, whether this is TV or cocaine.

Kubey said later that there wasn't really enough hard evidence to back up the claim that TV is clinically addictive, but it certainly captures our attention in ways that seem hard to withstand. Kubey and Csikszentmihalyi suggest that this is because TV completely engages our orienting response — an instinctive visual and auditory response to any sudden or new stimulus in our environment. If we hear a crash, we turn to look for it. If a moving object comes into our environment, we turn to look at it automatically. Infants have been shown to respond in the same way to TV, craning their necks around 180 degrees while lying on the floor, just trying to see, as Kubey and Csikszentmihalyi say, "what light through yonder window breaks."

This means that TV is appealing to a built-in sensitivity to movement that we developed in the far distant past in order

Although babies are drawn to look at a TV by the orienting response, which reacts to sound and visual changes, they do not continue to watch if the content is uninteresting to them.

to notice and track movement and so to stay alive. This would seem to be a pretty compelling reason to check out that flickering, noisy box in the corner. But why don't we switch it off, once we've realized it's not only not threatening, but not even particularly interesting?

Are there positives to watching soap operas?

Soap addicts might point out all sorts of ways in which TV soaps are interesting, relevant and informative. Teenagers claim that soaps give them a useful window onto the world of adults and so provide them with invaluable information. They like to reflect on how the social conflicts arising in series are dealt with by the various characters, and wonder how they might deal with these situations themselves. Like adult soap watchers, they also enjoy discussing the plots and characters with family and friends. This all adds up to a rich social experience, in terms of learning, imagining and actual socializing after the event with people in the real world.

The ancient Greek philosopher Aristotle was the first to point out that the human being is "by nature a social animal," and

> *"The orienting response is our instinctive visual or auditory reaction to any sudden or novel stimulus. It is part of our evolutionary heritage."*
> Kubey and Csikszentmihalyi

The need to complete

Gestalt psychologists have drawn attention to our need to complete things, from stories to shapes. Here you may see unified, complete shapes that are not provided on the page.

evolutionary social psychologists point out that humans have lived in small, kin-based groups for over three million years. They suggest that many of the ways in which we think and act have evolved to solve the problems of living in groups; people in all countries seem to have large vocabularies for describing the extent to which a person is cooperative or dominant, a potential leader, enemy or ally. In 1992 John Tooby and Lisa Cosmides showed that we're very good at solving difficult logical problems if they are reframed in ways that ask us to detect "cheaters" in social situations. In other words, we're fascinated by watching social interactions. There's even a theory — the *Machiavellian Intelligence Hypothesis* — that

suggests primate intelligence evolved primarily to deal with complex social problems, rather than for finding food or using tools.

Robin Dunbar's *Social Gossip Theory* says that language evolved in humans so that we could track complex social relationships and find ways to maintain them among large social groups. This suggests that it has always been so important to our survival to find ways to communicate with each other and live alongside one another that our language, behavior and even ways of thinking have developed largely around social interactions.

Dunbar's theory refers to just the kind of social information that teenagers describe themselves as extracting from soap operas.

"Finding a plausible explanation for the interruption did not, however, mean satisfaction with the fact of being interrupted. On the contrary. The subjects objected, sometimes quite strenuously."
Bluma Zeigarnik

> *"Television is going to be the test of the modern world ...
> we shall discover either a new and unbearable disturbance of the
> general peace or a saving radiance in the sky."*
> E.B. White

And there's no reason to assume that the rest of us aren't picking up some handy tips too, about the thinking and behavioral habits of people from different backgrounds and cultures, along with the many ways of looking at and solving social problems. In the same way that our orienting response is an ancient instinct that's caught by the flickering, noisy TV, our need to constantly increase our knowledge of social relationships and interactions is exerting an evolutionary pull.

In addition, there's one last thing that may be at play: the workings of human memory. In 1927 psychologist **Bluma Zeigarnik** described how, in one experiment after another, she found that if we are interrupted during a task and it is left unfinished, we enjoy a 90 percent memory advantage over people who complete the task. This explains how waiters in a restaurant are able to remember a whole table's orders without notes, but once the bill is paid, the information is forgotten. The human mind keeps the file open on memories where there is still something left to do (or find out). Zeigarnik's work led to the study of the human tendency to "resume" and the *Theory of Closure* (the need to get to the end).

Our intense dislike of stopping in the middle of something may also explain something of the hook of the serial, either in Victorian magazines, as for Charles Dickens, or for the modern soap opera on TV today. Zeigarnik found that her experimental subjects objected strongly to being interrupted — once something is begun, we want to find out how it ends. Especially when it is a story, and even more so if the story revolves around human relationships. In 1979 Owens, Bower and Black read people descriptions of a woman doing several tasks: making a cup of coffee, going to the doctor, buying milk, attending a lecture and going to a party. When one group of listeners was also told that the woman was pregnant by her professor, the description of her day was suddenly rich in connection and story and their memory of the events was significantly enhanced in comparison to a control group.

So it seems we're evolutionarily wired to respond to the thing that is the TV and the stories that never end. It's amazing that we find time to do anything else at all!

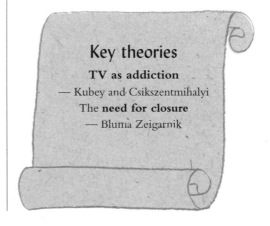

Key theories

TV as addiction
— Kubey and Csikszentmihalyi
The **need for closure**
— Bluma Zeigarnik

Why do I act like such an idiot in front of my partner's parents?

Erving Goffman • Donald Winnicott • Alice Miller

This sounds as though you're aware of playing a part, which means we turn first to Erving Goffman. Although he was a sociologist, his ideas were nonetheless key to the formation of drama therapy. Goffman said that it's a mistake to think of the self as an organic thing — it's nothing but a "dramatic effect" that arises from within a scene or context.

In *The Presentation of Self in Everyday Life,* **Goffman** pointed out that when an individual finds himself in the presence of strangers, those people will try to acquire information about him, and the more successful they are at doing this, the happier they will feel about knowing what is expected of them. We look for information like this from noticing someone's clothes, for instance, along with their accent, hairstyle, physical stance, facial expressions and so on. This is how we build up a picture of who this new person is, but Goffman points out that we have to accept this person on faith — we have to tell ourselves that he really is just like the person he is presenting himself as being.

At the same time, the individual wants something; he may want the new people he is meeting to think highly of him, or to believe that he thinks highly of them, or he may wish to confound all their expectations and remain somewhat mysterious. (All three of these may come into play in the meeting of a partner's parents.) Goffman points out that this is all about control: the newcomer wants to control the other people's conduct and their opinion of him. This means he might depart widely from his "natural" self, and present himself very differently from the way he behaves toward his friends, his partner, his teachers, his boss and so on. Each of us, according to Goffman, plays a part according to the situation in which we find ourselves. It is this ability to act "as if" that is used in drama therapy to free us from habitual ways of acting.

Goffman would not lay any personal blame at your door for "acting weirdly" with your partner's parents, because he says that society demands that we all act like this to keep the wheels of everyday life running smoothly. He also says that the idea that we would all present ourselves candidly and express what we really feel is an optimistic ideal and an unnecessary one. What the newcomer must do is keep everyone happy by conveying "a view of the situation which he feels the others will be able to find at least temporarily acceptable." Goffman suggests he does this by suppressing "his immediate heartfelt feelings."

Playing to the gallery

The idea that we play at being someone else to keep those around us happy

Life as a theatrical performance

Goffman says social behavior is a theatrical performance in front of an audience, with a stage, props and so on. For instance, in a restaurant, the dining area would be the "stage" where the waiter (actor) puts the script into action by handing you a menu (a prop) and asking for your order. Food (more props) are prepared in the kitchen (backstage) and the waiter delivers it with appropriate ceremony (definitely a performance!) before disappearing (off stage). You have been the audience member at the center of this entire production. But it's more complicated than that, because this is not just a performance in front of you, it involves you. So just as you have been an audience for the actor playing the waiter, he has also been your audience, while you have been playing the customer. Goffman says that from this perspective, society can be seen as one huge act of (mostly) cooperative ensemble theater.

The emergence of a false self

| The true self contains the potential for false selves | The false self is extracted from the true self and becomes the visible self |

reverberates throughout psychotherapy and psychoanalysis. The reason you may find yourself morphing into what you think is their idea of "the perfect partner" for their daughter is that you have had plenty of practice at acting the perfect son or daughter for your own parents. Some therapists would say that this is inevitably true of all of us, because we ensured the continuation of care from our parents by being lovable — a necessarily changing, subjective state depending on the meaning of "lovable" to those concerned.

Donald Winnicott claimed that when we have "good enough" parenting, we can develop an authentic self (though there's no guarantee that you wouldn't still fall prey to acting a role under pressure, such as when meeting your partner's parents). The baby under the care of a parent who favored his or her own wants and desires above the baby's needs soon learns to silence his own needs in order to become the baby that his parent would ideally like him to be. This is the beginning of the development of a "false self," which may develop to such an extent

that the real self becomes entirely hidden, both from other people and virtually from oneself. In this situation it is possible to build an otherwise entirely successful life, full of academic, career and financial success, while feeling like a fraud or phony and finding it hard to build meaningful relationships. This person, says Winnicott, has withdrawn so far from a fully embodied "aliveness" that he may feel as though he is asleep and sleepwalking through life.

Mistaken respect
The psychoanalyst **Alice Miller** picked up on this idea with a vengeance as she began to realize how many of her clients had been badly treated during childhood. At the same time, they clung loyally to the idea that their parents had been good people, and their lives had been all right, really. Miller suggested that in these cases loyalty stems from an unconscious fear of abandonment, with the "adult child" often waiting a whole lifetime for his or her parents' love, steadfastly maintaining the parents' goodness at the cost of their own. They must be "bad" and have

> *"The self, then, as a performed character, is not an organic thing that has a specific location, whose fundamental fate is to be born, to mature, to die: it is a dramatic effect arising diffusely from a scene that is presented."*
> Erving Goffman

deserved the punishments they received (see also how Dorothy Rowe connects a similar idea to depression, on pages 37–9).

Through therapy, Miller helped people unearth and reinterpret memories, in the process rediscovering their own true feelings, which had been put aside in order for the mythically happy family to keep functioning. Miller suggests we throw away the idea that we must "honor our father and our mother," unless they act in ways that are worthy of respect. Otherwise, she said, this idea can be used to destroy children, making them ignore their feelings to the point of being unable to know what they genuinely like or want any more, and leaving them with an inexplicable feeling of guilt that lasts for their entire lives.

So is it a problem?

It seems that the false self may be a crippling lifelong façade, or it may simply be a mask that is put on temporarily by an otherwise happy being in order to grease the wheels of social situations. Since you have an idea of "acting like an idiot," this suggests that you are not unknowingly living in a false self but find yourself occasionally putting on a protective disguise to fit the occasion. Goffman would suggest that you're understandably aiming for a "working consensus," because you have "motives for

trying to control the impression they receive of the situation." You want them to like you — not in a desperate way, but because it would be helpful. This is entirely natural and understandable, but you may find that you need to gently ease your true self into the room on future occasions. Freud might wonder about the need to please, though, and direct you to page 24.

Key theories
Life as performance
— Erving Goffman
False and true selves
— Donald Winnicott

Why do I keep buying the same brand all the time?

John B. Watson • Daniel Kahneman • Paul MacLean

The insidious power of marketing meets the irrational unconscious mind and suddenly there's a bar of chocolate in your hand. At least, that's what the neuromarketers would have everyone believe, but then they insist that our decisions are made by the "reptilian" part of our brain. Is our decision-making really that simple?

Psychology and advertising became working partners in 1922, when the advertising firm J. Walter Thompson hired the psychologist **John B. Watson**, now known as "the father of behaviorism," to advise them. Watson had recently become famous for showing that it was possible to induce a conditioned emotional reflex in animals and children. Building on Pavlov's work that demonstrated ways in which dogs could be made to behave in a certain way in response to a stimulus, Watson showed that people could be made to *feel* a certain way in response to a stimulus. This was a huge leap in understanding, and when Watson was fired from Johns Hopkins University for his scandalous divorce, J. Walter Thompson — one of the largest advertising agencies in the world — was happy to hire him.

Real features don't matter

Watson's task was to work out how to use psychology to persuade people to buy products. One of the first experiments he carried out along these lines investigated the power of brand loyalty (though the term had not yet been invented). He asked cigarette smokers to identify brands through smoking them, and discovered that they weren't even able to pick out their own brand. As a behaviorist, he was surprised; he had assumed people were conditioned to their chosen brand by taste and physiological effect. What he discovered instead was that brands evoke feelings and emotions in the consumer; people buy items not for their features but for their "atmosphere." His reasoning was that consumers have previously conditioned traits (such as being drawn to pictures of smiling faces or rolling countryside) and advertisers need only tap

> "I began to learn that it can be just as thrilling to watch the growth of a sales curve of a new product as to watch the learning curve of animals and men."
> John B. Watson

The triune brain

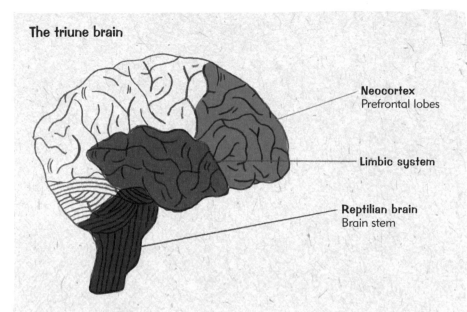

Neocortex
Prefrontal lobes

Limbic system

Reptilian brain
Brain stem

The human brain developed during evolution. The oldest part of the brain includes structures found in a reptilian brain. The limbic system shares mammalian structures and the neocortex first assumed importance in primates.

into these. In other words, instead of selling products by focusing on their features, advertisers should focus instead on imparting a message that appeals to the psychological traits of their consumers.

In a further development, Watson suggested that a successful brand is one that develops an image or personality that appeals to the conditioned desires of consumers — such as the conditioned (i.e. not inborn) desire for high status and wealth. So Maxwell House coffee, one of JWT's clients, produced advertisements in glorious settings, such as one that displays the actress Lily Langtry sipping Maxwell House coffee at a candelabra-adorned dinner table, accompanied by a gentleman in black tie

smoking a cigar. It was no longer about the product; advertisements now focused on what buying the product said about the consumer.

Hardwired to decide fast

Watson was clearly onto something. And that something is this: our brains are hardwired in such a way that we are subject to certain biases at an unconscious level. This is not Freud's idea of the unconscious (though he might argue that it is actually the same), but the "unconscious" as suggested by psychologists and neuroscientists today. Scientists, in other words. This is the lightning-fast System 1 suggested by **Kahneman** (see page 52), able to process

Neocortex
Newest part of brain.
Handles language and
consciousness.
Enables complex thinking.
Revises decisions made
by the rest of the brain.

Emotional brain
Produces emotional responses.
Connects information to memory.

Reptilian brain
Oldest part of brain.
Controls autonomic functions.
Drives fundamental needs.
Can't understand language.

evolved through evolutionary time, with three different eras of brain sitting one above the next. The oldest, lowest type of brain is called the "reptilian brain" — this controls autonomic functions (such as breathing) and drives fundamental needs like feeding, drinking, mating and, basically, surviving. This part of the brain does not learn from its mistakes; it tends to be rigid and compulsive. It takes in sensory information but can't understand language (so it doesn't respond to words in advertisements).

On top of this is the emotional brain or "limbic system" that we share with all mammals. This produces an emotional response to a stimulus, moving us away from painful things toward more pleasant ones, and it helps us learn from experience ("Mmm … that was delicious, I'll eat that again.") by connecting information to memory.

At the very top sits the neocortex — the newest part of the brain in terms of evolution. This is found in all mammals but is generally quite small except in humans, where it accounts for around 76 percent of the brain's volume. This part handles language and consciousness; it enables us to do complex thinking, calculations and, importantly, revise the decisions streaming up from the rest of the brain. It can override bias, given the chance (this is Kahneman's System 2; see page 52). Marketing, however, uses devices aimed at getting decisions out of us before we take that long or get that far, and neuromarketing claims it can pin down exactly how to do this, for every individual product.

around 10 quadrillion calculations every second, while passing an extremely limited number of thoughts through to our conscious mind for consideration. It needs to "think" fast, so it has shortcuts for doing this, which operate at all levels of the brain.

Neuroscientists have tried to simplify the basic workings of the human brain for the rest of us, by describing its three main processing areas within a model known as the "triune brain." This was devised by **Paul MacLean** to explain how the human brain

> *"We don't see with our eyes, we see with our brain"*
> Paul Bach-y-Rita

Can neuromarketing manipulate the brain?

Neuromarketing uses a variety of tools, such as brain scanning, eye-tracking, facial coding and biofeedback to measure how people *really* respond to products, rather than how they say that they do (because it turns out we often lie to market researchers — who knew?). They claim that this information can tell them how successful a product will be, based on the brain's involuntary responses. Some neuromarketers have suggested that this means they should steer marketing directly to the lowest level of the brain — the reptilian — because this is the first level of response, so it makes quick decisions (impulse buys). Marketers appeal to the reptilian brain by using messages encoded in visual images, not language (because the reptilian brain can't read); using a story (because the reptilian brain can't tell the difference between reality and a story); by appealing to innate selfishness and the move from pain toward pleasure; and by making a standout, obvious grab for attention.

Do reptiles form habits?

The reptilian brain might make us reach for our favorite chocolate bar, and the emotional brain is likely then to give us a kick of "I love these!" before possibly delivering a second response of guilt (over price, calories or some such) and oscillating between them. We might get to the till before reaching a rational response, which is why impulse buys often seem strange once we get home.

But habitual purchases do bring in some other factors that would appeal to our reptilian brain. We're hardwired to be wary of novelty; it attracts our attention, but it brings potential danger ("Is that stripey animal I've never seen before dangerous or not?") and slows us down, which is a problem when you're dealing with quadrillions of bits of data, so we feel safer with already-checked-out information. We also like to have our expectations met: the supermarket will be filled with food to buy, not live animals; a birthday party will be fun, not an endurance test. If our expectations are met, we're not threatened — the threat response is not triggered by a feeling of "What the heck?" We feel safe. And the human nervous system — including every part of the brain — loves a feeling of safety (or undisturbed *homeostasis*). Which may explain, ultimately, why that first bite of your favorite chocolate bar feels so good.

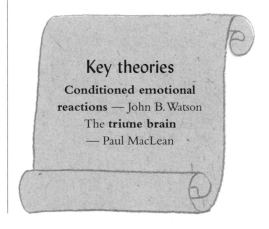

Key theories

Conditioned emotional reactions — John B. Watson

The **triune brain** — Paul MacLean

Other people

Page 86: Why can't I find Mr./Mrs. Right?

Page 91: Why is the new guy acting so friendly toward me?

Page 94: How do I stop my teenage daughter getting a tattoo?

Page 98: Why is my partner such a loser?

Page 103: My partner is great — so why am I thinking of having an affair?

Page 107: How can I stop people unfriending me on social media?

Page 110: Why is my boss always so mean?

Page 115: My family's a nightmare — shall I cut them off?

Page 119: Is my partner lying to me?

Page 123: My boss is so cool — she's quick, articulate, organized and even well dressed. Why aren't I like that?

Chapter 3

Why can't I find Mr./Mrs. Right?

Erich Fromm

This is surely one of the most common and heartfelt of questions. It feels as though finding love should be easy — judging from all the online dating ads, the search for love is just like buying a house: see as many as you can, especially those that fall within a bracket that suits your needs, and you're bound to come up with the perfect match. Apparently it's all about data — specify what you're looking for, keep up the numbers and all will come good. So is it just that you're not trying hard enough?

The psychoanalyst **Erich Fromm** would be horrified by this approach, and he was something of an expert on love. In *The Art of Loving*, published in 1957, he said that we're looking at this in entirely the wrong way, mainly because "our whole culture is based on the appetite for buying." This means that we think that if we look in enough shop windows we'll find the perfect person and that will be that. This carries with it a number of strange assumptions, he says, not least that the other person is a desirable "object." We seem to be saying that true love occurs when two people feel they have found the best object available on the market.

If this seems harsh, that's all to the good, as far as Fromm is concerned, because he thinks

we are sleepwalking to eternal isolation. The commodifying of relationships is not making for a better world or happier people. We're acting narcissistically when we assume that it's a question of being loved, rather than loving. It also means that we feel obliged to make ourselves suitable objects of love by amassing cash, status and cosmetically enhanced good looks. Then there's the strange way in which we assume it's all about an object (finding the right person) rather than mastering a skill — the ability to love and be loving. People think that to love is simple, Fromm says, but finding a love object is hard, when actually it's the other way around. Why else would there be so many failed relationships? Loving

"Love is not primarily a relationship to a specific person: it is an attitude, an orientation of character."

Erich Fromm

Fromm's evolution of the productive self

| Don't be purely receptive | Don't become hoarding | Don't be exploitative |

is an art, that requires mastering just as much as music, painting or carpentry, and it requires dedication.

Surely love is a natural thing?

Absolutely. The problem is that our idea of love has been distorted by both consumerist cultures and misleading myths about there being a "one" who's out there waiting to be found. There's a popular ancient myth, referred to in Plato's *Symposium*, that humans used to be perfectly happy spherical beings with eight limbs and two sets of genitals, but one day they displeased the gods and so Zeus cut each of them in half, with the result that everyone is still looking for their other half. This myth of how finding your "perfect match" guarantees a happy ending can be heard in fairy tales around the world,

embedding the belief in our psyches. But Fromm, ever the realist, says that this is a very strange idea. It's like an artist not bothering to learn how to paint, because she assumes that, when the perfect object or model turns up, she'll be able to paint beautifully. What has happened to our sense of agency, beyond going shopping?

It's all about me

We need to stop being so narcissistic ("Look at me, aren't I lovely?") and materialistic ("He ticks all the right boxes, I'll have him.") and take a long hard look at where this need for love is coming from, according to Fromm. Because, essentially, it's about the acute loneliness of the human condition. We are born alone, will die alone, and our friends and loved ones will die both before and after

> "It's not ... the gimmick of how do you get your boyfriend to pay more attention to you ... It's how can I enlarge my sensitivity, my capacity to love?"
> Rollo May

Don't see people as commodities	Value life above objects	Be truly independent

us. We are not only separate from every other living being, but aware of it too, and in this we are unique among the animals on Earth.

So here's what we should do, he says. Love is the only power that can break through the walls that separate each of us from each other, but for true intimacy to occur — a true meeting of minds, souls and bodies — the union must be of two evolved or Productive selves. This is the highest form of personality type for Fromm, who identified six personality orientations, five of which can lead only to unhappiness. If you want to experience true love, don't be a Receptive type, he warns, expecting everything to land on your plate and for others to take responsibility for you. This is the route to a masochistic relationship. Resist the urge to become Hoarding and see everything — even people and ideas — as possessions. Don't

be Exploitative in your approach, entering relationships only when they allow you to manipulate the other person toward your own ends (this way lies sadism). Avoid the oh-so-common Marketing orientation, where "new is beautiful" and all problems are simply manifestations of the market. Partners are not there just to make you look good. Lastly, don't fall prey to becoming Necrophilous, fascinated by death and dead things, or the purely mechanistic/technological world with its imitations of life. Love requires a commitment to living in the fullest sense.

Love in abundance

The only type of person who will be capable of mastering the art of loving, says Fromm, is the Productive person, who lives "without a mask." This person is not chained by the artificial customs and compulsions of

> *"A wonderful living side by side can grow, if they succeed in loving the distance between them which makes it possible for each to see the other whole and against a wide sky."*
> R.M. Rilke

> *"Sexual attraction creates, for the moment, the illusion of union, yet without love this 'union' leaves strangers as far apart as they were before."*
> Erich Fromm

society, and responds in an open, flexible and interested way to challenges. He or she has no fear of accepting people for who they are and accepting them completely. In love, this person is entirely giving, but does not in any way feel this to be a sacrifice. Giving is the highest expression of potency, according to Fromm; in the very act of giving we experience our strength, our wealth and our power.

It is this desire to give and share — our joy, our interest, our understanding, our knowledge, our humor, our sadness — that is the true motivation for love. We will treat the other person with care, respond to their needs and always treat them with respect. "Respect" in this context returns the word to its Latin roots: *respicere*, "to look at," because we need to be able to see the other person exactly as he is, not as we wish to see him, and help him "grow and unfold" in his own way. Lastly, we must be prepared to come to know the other person at the deepest level, so that when she is angry, we know that she is also anxious and worried, and feels lonely, so that we can see the suffering of the other person, rather than react to her as simply "angry."

In order to be like this, we must have developed into truly independent people, able to walk "without needing crutches, without having to dominate and exploit anyone else." Without looking for Mr. or Mrs. Right. The search for love stems from an intense awareness of loneliness, and yet, paradoxically, says Fromm, the ability to be alone is the prerequisite condition for the ability to love.

So should I stop looking?

Fromm would suggest stopping the search for Mr. or Mrs. Right until you realize that you no longer need to look for someone — you're fine on your own. Only then might you be ready to love someone. "Mature love," he writes, "is union under the condition of preserving one's integrity, one's individuality ... In love the paradox occurs that two beings become one and yet remain two." If that gives you pause, he might add that "analytic therapy is essentially an attempt to help the patient gain or regain his capacity for love ..." and with a kindly smile, guide you once more toward the couch.

Key theories
The **art of loving**
— Erick Fromm

Why is the new guy acting so friendly toward me?

Sigmund Freud

Friendliness does not usually concern us, but there is a slight anxiety or puzzlement behind your question; the friendliness seems to you undeserved or unsupported by adequate interpersonal history. It's possible that an erotic attraction is driving the friendliness, but it's unlikely that you would be puzzled if this were the case — unless you are reacting in a similar way without knowing it. Ah, says Freud, rubbing his hands with glee. The unconscious at work. Perhaps the new guy sees you as his mother?

Freud would be the first to agree that reality is a tricky thing to pin down. Philosophers have known this for millennia and point to the fact that we only have our five senses to give us a sense of what's "out there" beyond our bodies. With another five, we might be perceiving and experiencing the world quite differently. Freud would not argue with that, but he would want to add a few more layers of difficulty. Information from our senses is interpreted by our brains and this interpretation depends upon the way that we have learned to organize experience. That is to say, the way that each of us, personally, has come to understand the world will affect what we perceive and what we take it to mean. Events, places and even things mean different things to different people.

The author Anaïs Nin illustrates this beautifully in a passage from *Seduction of the Minotaur*. "Together they would walk along the same Seine river — she would see it silky grey, sinuous and glittering, he would draw it opaque with fermented mud, and a shoal of wine bottle corks and weeds caught in the stagnant edges." As the saying from the Talmud goes: "We do not see things as they are. We see things as we are."

Building templates

Just to complicate things further, Freud would say that we are not even aware of "how we see things" half the time, because we banish so many of our thoughts from consciousness (see page 12). There's also the fact that we interpret all our relationships with other people according to interpersonal "templates" that we drew up as children, when we were first learning how to survive in the world. Babies are helpless, so survival depends on receiving continuing care from adults; as a result, infants quickly learn what effect their own behaviors have on each of the people around them (getting this wrong may result in a survival threat). Infants also have needs for tenderness, connection and self-expression, all of which require the active involvement of another person, so mastering the art of relationship is fundamental to a child's continuing health and development. As the psychotherapist Richard Erskine says, the central question for a child is this: "What does someone like me do, with people like you, in a world like this?" In working this out, we build templates for relationships with our initial caregivers that we will bring into play with all our subsequent relationships, unless the templates are made conscious and disrupted in some way.

Transference

The templates (Freud called them "stereotype plates") govern both how we see and act with other people and the expectations we have of them. For instance, if your father was severe and critical, you might find yourself assuming all sorts of things when you meet your boss for the first time, and he's around 20 or 30 years older than you. You might assume that he's judging you and already holds you in low esteem, which in turn makes you feel and act defensively. If he does say something that sounds slightly negative, you might find yourself thinking that this is never going to work out and wishing that you'd never taken the job. This is not madness — it's a process that Freud called *transference*, whereby we take the feelings and expectations we had toward a significant person in our past and transfer them onto

someone else in the present. Essentially, we take a relationship template and stick it onto a new person.

This is not quite as strange as it first appears. Contemporary research using a social-cognitive model has also demonstrated that mental representations of significant people are stored in memory (Freud's "templates") and can be activated and applied in new social encounters. Professor Susan Andersen has found that when we meet a new person who activates a significant-other representation, we not only infer traits about them for which there is no evidence — we also then treat these traits as though they were really learned about that person, and bundle them into our memory of the person along with the real traits and characteristics.

This doesn't stop with simply mis-seeing and misremembering people. Andersen notes that a "whole variety of complex affects, motivations, expectancies, behaviors and self-changes may occur in relation to this new person — based on the transference process." Her experiments suggest that the process of transference is triggered in everyday interpersonal relations, and is so ubiquitous that it may occur based on the

"Psychoanalysis does not create [transference] but merely reveals it to consciousness and gains control of it in order to guide psychical processes toward the desired goal."
Sigmund Freud

92

representations of various significant others, including siblings, best friends and partners, as well as parents.

If this is correct, we are all operating with a range of templates that we bring into play all the time. That new woman at the school gate that you feel like you already know? Perhaps she looks like your sister or your old best friend. It may be her smile, a gesture she makes with her hand or the way she stands and frowns at her watch. If your mind notices enough visual or auditory traits in common with someone important from your past, it will trigger the same feelings in you toward this new person.

So, that new guy in the office may be looking at you and experiencing just this. Perhaps you have an easy laugh and like to sit halfway on a desk chatting, just like his best friend at school. Or perhaps he's noticed you offering people coffee and talking earnestly to people about their bad day, like his mum always did. He won't know any of this, of course, because it's unconscious. He just knows that he feels friendly toward you for some reason. Negative transference emerges

as feelings of hostility, but this sounds like a case of positive transference, which Freud said was all to the good because it helped his clients stay attached to the analytic process. Positive transference always carries feelings of warm attachment, so it's good for forming alliances. Which is always useful in competitive settings, like the workplace and far cheaper for the company than sending you off on luxury team-building courses. No need to tell them that though. Enjoy.

Key theories

Transference
— Sigmund Freud
Significant-other representation
— Susan Andersen

How do I stop my teenage daughter getting a tattoo?

Daniel Siege • Peter Huttenlocher

As the neuroscientist and psychiatrist Daniel Siegel says, "Life is on fire when we hit our teens." Taking adolescence as the period between 12 and 24 years of age, he says that during this time, changes in the brain steer the teenager toward four hard-to-handle things: novelty seeking, increased emotional intensity, creative exploration and intense social engagement, especially with peers. That's hard to handle from both sides of the child–parent relationship, and how better to kick-start the challenge than by getting a tattoo — as your daughter wants to do?

Siegel is a big fan of teenagers, whom he sees as having to negotiate both mind and body changes while forming an identity within a particular family and culture. But most importantly, he says, this is the time at which brave, innovative thinking — which we need in our future adult generations — is either crushed or fostered. If we can help teenagers safely seek out new experiences, handle emotional intensity, experiment with creative impulses and engage in meaningful ways socially, they will live fuller lives as teenagers and as adults. If we can't, and these four impulses are lost during adolescence, their lives as adults will be boring, lackluster, routine-filled and lonely. In addition, everyone will just carry on using the same old-world strategies of previous generations, which is not useful in a changing world. In the "adapt or die" realities of evolution, Siegel says, adolescents are our adaptive force. We need their keen impulse toward challenge and change, but we also need to stay sane ourselves while helping them negotiate this great period of change.

Give me a reward!

Having laid his cards on the table, Siegel explains why all this change is happening. During adolescence there is an increase in the neural circuits of the brain that utilize dopamine, a neurotransmitter (brain chemical) that plays a central part in creating our drive for reward. As children hit their teens, dopamine release is steadily enhanced until it reaches a peak level at about the age of 18. This change in the brain causes teenagers to gravitate toward thrilling experiences and sensations which will release dopamine. Some research suggests that the base rate of dopamine in teenagers actually sits lower than normal, but rises much higher than for the rest of us in response to an exhilarating experience, which may explain why the most common moan of the teenager on a normal day is "I'm soooo bored."

The increased drive toward the feeling of reward manifests itself in three important ways, says Siegel: impulsiveness, increased susceptibility to addiction and hyperrationality. The dopamine-driven impulse demands instant gratification; there's no time to think before you act, hence impulsiveness — get that thrill, take that risk, right now! Or take the shortcut to dopamine by ingesting an addictive substance, having sex or hanging out in the mosh pit, because drink, drugs, sex and rock 'n' roll (most forms of music, in fact) lead to the release of dopamine. The bad news is that within a few hours the dopamine level plummets, sending the user back for another hit. Lastly, *hyperrationality* is the word Siegel uses to refer to a teenager's sudden switch to a very literal way of thinking, where the facts of "right here and now" are everything and the context is irrelevant. He suggests that this way of thinking comes from a brain calculation that places a lot of weight on the potential positive results ("It will be thrilling!") and little on the negative ones ("It's extremely dangerous.").

Laying down the fast track

As we approach the end of adolescence, we begin to take in the bigger picture and consider the wider consequences and longer-term gains (or losses) of our actions. This happens because the brain goes through an integration process during adolescence that results from

Much as Michelangelo's carving revealed the beautiful *David* as he chipped away at it, so the human brain reaches its most effective form by the pruning of neural connections during the teenage years. This leaves the most used and useful to be coated in a myelin sheath that protects them and increases our speed of thought.

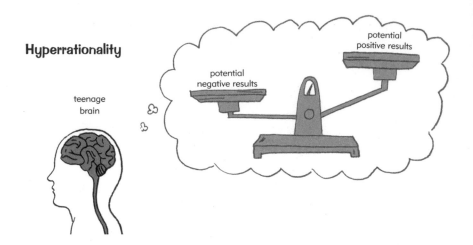

two things: a very thorough pruning of neural connections and the laying down of myelin, creating a protective sheath around nerves. In 1979, neuroscientist **Peter Huttenlocher** showed that during childhood we produce lots and lots of neurons and their synaptic connections, but at the age of around 12 we prune away all the excess connections — the ones we don't use — so that we've got a faster, more effective brain. For instance, if you learned the flute aged 7 but only played it for a year, the neural circuits involved with flute playing will be pruned away. If you continued to play it from the age of 7 onward, the circuits won't be pruned but strengthened; the brain will cover the membranes between interlinked neurons with a myelin sheath. This allows the faster and more coordinated flow of information along that route, making the circuit quicker and more effective.

During this remodeling the brain can be thought of as a building site, where the plumbing, electricity and so on will be great one day, but they're currently on hold. The reconstruction of the prefrontal cortex means that the great things it will be able to do once the brain is fully integrated again — such as balancing emotions, planning for the future, making decisions and having empathy and insight — are fragile at best and often don't seem to be working at all.

Self-awareness comes online, together with abstract thinking, but it's coupled with the emotional intensity of this period, so even though these are higher cortex activities, they can be experienced as "too much." At the same time, the lower areas below the cortex become more active, especially the amygdala, which assesses level of threat in the environment. Usually we have access to two routes for information to the amygdala: the slow route, via the

> *"Adolescents are our future, and it is through their courage and their sometimes outrageous but creative efforts 'not to be like everyone else' that our species has been adaptive."*
> Daniel Siegel

higher cortex, which has already sifted the incoming information, and the fast route, where incoming streams of perception go straight to the amygdala. Studies have shown that the fast route occurs much more often in teens than adults, meaning that intense emotions from the amygdala may fire up over the most innocent of remarks.

The "social engagement" that Siegel says becomes very important to teens and their peers stems from an evolutionary instinct that all mammals possess, which assumes that there is safety in groups. For humans, admission to a group depends on fulfilling certain requirements, such as having long hair and wearing lots of makeup, or skateboarding for six hours a day, or opting for black hair and clothes and covering yourself in piercings.

So what about the tattoo?

Getting a tattoo may be about social engagement, because it may be part of the "uniform" that your daughter sees in a group that she wishes to join. It's also something new and different, so it will appeal to the novelty seeking that's driving her at the moment, and it may look to her like creative exploration, as she seeks the most interesting way to decorate her body and to play with her physical identity. I'm guessing your instinct is to appeal to the reasoning power of her prefrontal cortex about the wisdom of this over the longer

term, but that's not working well right now as it undergoes the pruning process (plus you'll be stressing the risk, which will be actively appealing to her). It's also likely that any input from you will be interpreted immediately via the amygdala as a threat ("Back off! Stop interfering with my life!").

Your best hope of success lies in coaxing the cortex back into operation as best it can while soothing the amygdala, by keeping communications open, calm and positive, according to Siegel. And perhaps use that old toddler trick of diversion: how else might she satisfy her needs for new, thrilling experiences, close friendships and emotional intensity? I'll leave that one with you.

Key theories

The **teenage brain**
— Daniel Siegel
Synaptic pruning
— Peter Huttenlocher

Why is my partner such a loser?

John Bowlby • Mary Ainsworth • Donald Winnicott • Judith Solomon • Mary Main

It seems there's no getting away from the fact that the partners we pick reflect something about our earliest relationships. From Freud's suggestion along these lines back in the 1890s to today's modern attachment theorists this rule holds good; apparently we will replay the dynamics we experienced as infants when we choose partners as adults. These working models dictate not only whom we choose, but how we see our partners, and it's this that is relevant here. Why would you have a partner that you view as being "a loser"?

It might seem like a huge leap to accept that the way we related to our parents continues to haunt us in very specific ways, but there is a huge amount of evidence, gathered from many countries, that now backs up the central notion of *attachment theory*. This claims that the everyday way that our parents responded to us, and our responses in turn toward them, essentially form a working model or template for all our later relationships. Freud had claimed that these relationships were important, but in the 1960s researchers began to find that the actual moment-to-moment interactions that we have with parents as babies sets our relational interactions for life.

Freud and most of his followers believed that the child's internal fantasies about the external world played a significant part in the formation of their relational templates, but in the 1960s psychiatrist **John Bowlby** broke with this tradition and insisted that it is the reality (not fantasy) of what passes between children and their parents that makes a difference. He suggested that an attachment bond with evolutionary significance forms between caregiver and child, based on the detail of their interactions. This idea was furthered and tested in laboratory settings by his colleague, developmental psychologist **Mary Ainsworth**, who found that the style of attachment bond that develops is likely to be one of three types: Secure, Avoidant/Dismissing or Ambivalent.

Both baby and caregiver have a role to play in the kind of bond formed, because caregivers treat babies in ways that reflect their own psychological state and makeup, while babies respond to the care that is offered. Researcher Alison Gopnik suggests that babies are the Research and Development Department of the human race, because they are constantly formulating and testing hypotheses to find out what works in this new world in which they find themselves. They test out all sorts of things, but first and foremost they establish what they need to do to survive. So, if crying, for instance, results in food and a comforting hug, crying will stay among usable strategies. If it results in being ignored, or worse —

perhaps hit or shaken — crying will stop being a usable strategy, and the baby will learn to stay silent regardless of its needs. In this way, over a short space of time, infants adapt to their caregivers in ways that will keep the bond in place and allow at least the barest of survival needs to be met.

The reason that all this is important to us as adults is that these early interactions encode in the neural circuitry of our brains. This is because they are repeated daily, and as the psychologist Donald Hebb said in the 1940s, "Neurons that fire together wire together." This means we create fast neural pathways around everything to do with relationships. By 12–18 months of age, our patterns of attachment have become the "rules" or templates for how to relate to people and they will operate for our entire lives, unless at some point they are consciously disrupted. They run in our unconscious (or "implicit memory") like the background operating program of a computer, telling us how we should act in relationships and what to expect from other people who are close to us.

Happy days
Where parents are attuned, responsive and giving, infants learn that it is fine to express their needs and to expect them to be met. As

they get a little older, they find that sometimes they have to wait (no parent is perfect), and that's fine too. As the psychoanalyst **Donald Winnicott** pointed out, it's actually important for parents to fail in tolerable ways every now and then so that children learn how to live in an imperfect world. If the parents are "good enough" (responding flexibly and sensitively at least 40 percent of the time), the child will develop a secure sense of self and an independence that allows for further exploration. They're said to have developed a Secure attachment style.

Insecure in relationship
However, when parents are unable to respond easily and sensitively to their children, babies will start to pay more attention to their parents' needs than their own. This results in the insecure attachments of Ambivalent and Dismissing recognized by Ainsworth, and a fourth style, Disorganized, first suggested by **Judith Solomon** and **Mary Main** in the 1980s. Herein lies our answer, in all probability, because, while it's not possible to comment on whether your partner is "a loser" or not, what we do know is that you are in a relationship with someone that you feel able to refer to as "a loser." And since a relationship between two secure adults will be equal, honest, open,

"Parenting is not simply a set of behaviors, but participation in an interpersonal, diffuse, affective relationship."
Nancy Chodorow

Attachment styles

Secure

Find it relatively easy to get close to others • Tend to be more satisfied in their relationships than insecure adults • Feel confident that partners will be there when needed • Comfortable about being depended on or asking for help • Relationships characterized by greater longevity, trust, commitment and interdependence • Expect to be treated well and treat other people well • Have a noticeable capacity to connect

Ambivalent (in adults, this is also known as Anxious–preoccupied)

Worry that others may not love them completely • Easily frustrated or angered when their attachment needs go unmet • Continue to reexperience past hurts and rejections in a way that suggests they were never resolved • Like to stir things up and often sabotage relationships • Feel that others don't get as close to them as they want • Crave intimacy but doubt their own worth, so are suspicious of proffered intimacy • Require constant reassurance of partner's love

trusting and understanding, it would not tend to generate this kind of perspective. This form of relationship is the one that Erich Fromm (see page 88) suggested we aim for — one where each partner is truly independent; happy and relaxed in the other's company without any agenda.

Unfortunately, only around 50–60 percent of any population can be considered to have a Secure attachment style, leaving the rest of us insecure in some way — and with the possibility of throwing the words "you're a loser" at our partners.

Feeling ambivalent

If you were bought up by caregivers who were highly inconsistent or overly protective, you wouldn't have been able to relax in the same way that a secure child would have done. Researchers have found that children in this kind of relationship begin to work really hard to keep the attachment in place. They stay as close as possible to their caregiver, respond fairly dramatically when in trouble (to send a strong enough signal to get the caregiver's attention) and constantly need reassurance. These children are said to have an Ambivalent attachment style. As adults, they tend to connect with partners through helplessness, because this is what worked as a child. They might look resourceful and accomplished, but within an established relationship a pattern of appearing to be helpless will emerge, along with a desire to please.

People with this attachment style often feel a kind of emotional hunger that can never be

Avoidant (in adults, this is also known as Dismissive–avoidant)

Appear not to care too much about relationships • Avoid intimacy and conflict • Find it difficult to be close to others, trust them or depend on them • If others get close, experience a need to get away • Think of themselves as self-sufficient • Idealize previous romantic relationship so that current partner fails to live up to this • Likely to blame partner for relationship failure while actually suffering from extreme feelings of low self-worth

Disorganized

Have trouble making sense of their own experiences • Tend to run hot and cold in relationship • May soothe troubled feelings by harmful methods such as alcohol or drugs • Have trouble trusting people • Struggle to make sense of or maintain relationships • Afraid of closeness • Feel unworthy of love or support • Disregard rules and find dealing with authority figures very difficult • Have problems regulating emotions

satiated. Desperate for love, they nonetheless don't really trust their partner, and often become clingy, demanding and possessive, fearing always that their partner is about to leave them. The ambivalence (inconsistency) of the original relationship carries through into a push–pull style in adult relations — they long for safety and security but do things that push their partner away. Might this person call their partner a loser? Yes, in a pushing-away stage of the relationship. If you feel the need to grab back your partner even as you push them away with the "loser" comment, this may be where you stand, unable to relax in a relationship.

Feeling nothing

Children of parents who were unable to be emotionally available at all — who offered physical but not emotional sustenance — learn to take care of their own needs and not bother other people with them. After a while, they cease even to notice these needs, becoming blind to them and also dismissive, claiming not to have any feelings. As adults, they have one foot in and one foot out when it comes to relationships, and are afraid of intimacy or closeness; acknowledging the need for help would feel like an invitation to rejection or a humiliating admission of not being good enough in some way. The one feeling that's allowed, because it creates distance, rather than closeness, is anger. The psychotherapist David Wallin refers to adults with this relational style as "the merger wary who sabotage love." They grew up in an emotional desert, he says, and they have learned to shield themselves from

> *"Behind the mask of indifference is bottomless misery and behind callousness, despair."*
> John Bolwby

their own feelings and needs by thinking too well of themselves and too badly of others. They might well, in fact, be tempted to call their partner "a loser." The rule here is to keep a distance at all costs. Might this be your attachment style?

Feeling afraid

The fourth category of attachment, Disorganized, describes a bond between parent and child that is ambivalent but also dangerous, so that the child is both drawn to the parent for survival reasons, but at the same time fears to go near the parent because he or she constitutes a threat to survival. As adults they want to be close to other people, but fear getting hurt. They have difficulty controlling their emotions, because they had no help toward mastering this in childhood, so they are unpredictable in mood and behavior, just as their parents were. Might this person describe their partner as "a loser"? Yes. Would they dare? Possibly not, except perhaps during one of the rockier moments that this relationship would regularly visit. Or in their own heads, where the comment is just as likely then to turn inward as a painful criticism of themselves.

So now I'm more worried about me …

The good news is that secure attachment can be "earned," as psychotherapists say. This means that with determination, fearless self-awareness, honesty, lots of work and great feedback from people in close relationship to us (including a therapist), the original pattern can be identified, undone and knitted back together differently. With the deeper understanding that this brings, as well as a genuinely stronger sense of self, none of us would see someone as simply "a loser."

It's as though you've been taking a higher or lower pedestal than your partner for no reason other than old programming, and now you've leveled the playing field. Finally, you'll have a clear view of the world and a realization that you are, genuinely, OK, regardless of what other people think or do. As the psychotherapist Eric Berne would say, we're aiming for a position of thinking "I'm OK, you're OK." Lots of us are struggling with the legacy of our past and the challenges of the present, but we'll know we're collectively getting somewhere when we can all agree that no one's "a loser."

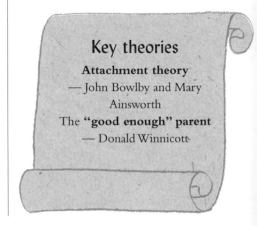

Key theories
Attachment theory
— John Bowlby and Mary Ainsworth
The **"good enough" parent**
— Donald Winnicott

My partner is great — so why am I thinking of having an affair?

Sigmund Freud • Jaak Panksepp • Daniel Kahneman

Herein lies the beauty and tragedy of being human. We're animals, and we share much of our brain structures and processes with other mammals, but we also have a far larger neocortex, which provides us with a self-awareness unique to the human race. So you and I have irrational animal impulses and desires, but also a rational part that says, "What the heck is going on?" Why doesn't rationality win the day?

Whether we talk in terms of **Freud**'s unconscious or the "implicit memory" of neuroscience, almost everyone seems to agree now that there are large parts of the human brain that run on autopilot in some way — that's to say, they are not under the control of the conscious mind. From Freud's unconscious (see page 11) to Kahneman's System 1 (see page 52) and **Panksepp**'s primary processes (see page 50), it seems that much of our decision-making takes place out of awareness, and as Kahneman notes, it's only when we begin to become aware of the biases allowing this fast processing to take place that we can begin to exert a more conscious control over our everyday lives.

Learning to be unfaithful

The human brain can't possibly process all its incoming stimuli consciously, so it operates under all sorts of *heuristics*, or rules of thumb, that allow our conscious attention to remain on what seems to be most important at any given time. One of these processes is known as *habituation*, and it's an important learning tool for humans and animals. Dog owners understand all

about habituation — it's the process that introduces dogs over and over again to certain things (such as small and noisy children) so that they are no longer bothered by the situation and in fact barely notice those stimuli after a while (so they no longer chase the children). Humans do this too: when something new comes into our environment we attend to it for a while (is it safe or is it threatening in some way?) before getting used to it (oh, it's only that car backfiring again) and effectively becoming oblivious to it. Habituation is a really useful tool for knowing what to safely ignore and what to pay attention to, but there's a bit of a downside for our partners. We become habituated to them, too. And blind to their charms, which once so attracted us.

Wow! What's that?

At the same time, we're inextricably drawn toward novelty, because dopamine levels in the brain increase in the context of novelty and this acts to push us toward the new thing in search of a "reward." It's the same neurotransmitter that plays a key part in addiction, pushing the addict toward the

Affordances

What does this thing do?

What can this person offer me?

We naturally scan our surroundings for affordances — things that may be useful to us — from a very early age. When we spot one, we are evolutionarily wired to take action.

reward of another high. When we spot something entirely new, we experience a similar rush — might there be a reward for me here? We get so excited by novelty that the mere possibility of finding new things motivates us to explore our environment, and this reveals its true evolutionary purpose — to help us discover new resources, like food and drink.

So we're hardwired to seek novelty and stop paying attention to the things (or people) that have been around us for a while — because they are not a threat and (brace yourselves) because we no longer associate them with reward: they have officially "lost their potential." Our brains assume that we've already reaped whatever reward might be gained from these "objects

"We are not thinking machines that feel — we are feeling machines that think."
Antonio Damasio

> *"When triggered, [the SEEKING system] merely looks for something in a nonspecific way. All that it seems to know is that the 'something' it wants is 'out there.'"*
> Mark Solms

in our environment" and we've stopped investigating them. (This is an assumption that might be worth a little conscious curiosity.)

What's out there for me?

Our vision is bound up with the eternal (unconscious) need for finding more resources. Babies are born with poor visual acuity, but after a while they begin to be able to see shapes and colors, and learn to differentiate one object from another, judge distances between objects and so on. This developmental gain allows the child to extract information from life or her surroundings and consider its "affordances" — the things it offers or provides which might be of use. It means a child can spot an apple on the ground and realize that food is on offer — and in this way the affordances are also opportunities for action. The child can reach out, pick up the apple and eat it. The long and short of this is that we're scanning our environment all the time, not only for potential threat, but also for potential rewards, including sex. If we find them, we're hardwired to take action — and you've just spotted an extremely good-looking person in the office kitchen who looks completely different from everyone else who works here.

Hardwired to explore

At this point, you're motivated to explore, because the SEEKING system of the brain

has come into play. The neuroscientist Jaak Panksepp discovered that within the 300-million-year-old mammalian part of our brain, we have seven primary-process emotional systems. These are neural circuits that are so identifiable that if one is stimulated using electrical brain stimulation, the emotion linked to that circuit, such as RAGE, is instantly evoked (see page 51). These are hardwired processes of enormous power, and the SEEKING system is perhaps the most important of all. This system (Panksepp uses capital letters to denote his particular uses of everyday words) is the one that keeps us up and about in the world. It gets us out of bed in the morning (What's the time? Where's my phone?) and motivates us; it impels us to constantly look out for useful information, people and objects. It's what makes a dog explore a new area expectantly, sniffing, digging into things, all the while expecting to turn up something great — and it may produce the same response in you when you spot the new person turning on the kettle at work. Hey what's that over there? That looks great! As you get closer you may feel the pull of another subcortical system: LUST. This is associated with consummation of the appetites that activated the SEEKING system. Uh oh.

Feeling really alive

The SEEKING system keeps us looking — for novelty, for resources, for life. The feelings associated with SEEKING are

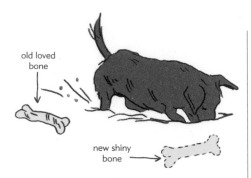

old loved bone

new shiny bone

enthusiasm, expectancy and hope. When people have suffered a difficult attachment as children (see pages 98–102), they feel less free to explore; their SEEKING system is turned down and may at times run toward the opposite end of this emotional continuum, toward depression. At one end lies despair, and at the other, huge feelings of expectancy, as though today you're going to find everything you ever wanted. If your SEEKING system goes up one gear from the novelty-induced dopamine, it steps up another once you decide to go and explore (that good-looking person in the kitchen), because this system sends dopamine to four different parts of the brain. So now you're on your way to the kitchen, hope, expectancy and enthusiasm for life riding high. You've "never felt so alive," right?

Is this a done deal?

Not at all, because otherwise you wouldn't have even asked your question, which illustrates the cognitive executive functions of the neocortex in play. These allow us to engage in independent, purposeful and "goal-directed behavior" — conscious goals,

that is, not unconscious ones. It means that we get to choose, not to simply react. The human part of the brain gives us all the powers we need to overcome the hardwired SEEKING for novelty, even with its oh-so-tempting dopamine hits. You have access to a full and amazing human mind, with powers that raise it far above other animals; a mind that holds memories, values, hopes and fears from the past, present and future, and knows not just lust, but love … and loss. So even if your feet begin to carry you toward a new attraction, keep all your brain in gear. Slow down. Question that dull feeling of habituation. Is all that glitters really gold, or is the dopamine affecting your eyesight? Pause. As with RAGE (see page 51), there's a moment of imminent danger. Catch it if you can.

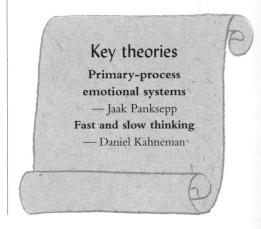

Key theories

Primary-process emotional systems
— Jaak Panksepp
Fast and slow thinking
— Daniel Kahneman

How can I stop people unfriending me on social media?

Albert Ellis

We are all a jumble of needs and wants, and one of the things we really want is for everybody to like us. Another thing most of us would like is more control over our lives, and it's a short step from here to realizing that we'd really like to make everyone like us. If this sounds a little like a toddler tantrum coming on, Albert Ellis would say that sounds about right. We've gone back to magical thinking and lost sight of rationality, which he thought could always step in to put things right. Forget about controlling the world, he'd say, and focus on thinking straight.

Ellis was an American psychoanalyst who lost faith in the ability of analysis to make a difference in people's lives. If Freud had a gene for inefficiency, he said, "I think I have it pure for efficiency." He wanted therapy to be more effective, so that people could experience a change in their lives quickly. He called his treatment *Rational Therapy* (clear and to the point, as ever), but it was perceived as ignoring feelings, so he renamed it *Rational Emotive Therapy*. Other professionals saw this as being "too cognitive" and ignoring behaviorism (even though it used many behavioral techniques), so once again Ellis caved in, renaming his therapy *Rational Emotive Behavior Therapy* (REBT).

Logical thinking

If Aaron Beck (see page 29) is the father of *Cognitive Behavioral Therapy*, Albert Ellis is considered the grandfather. Ellis suggested that we all hold a set of assumptions about ourselves, other people and the world in general, some of which are incorrect and irrational. Since these assumptions guide us throughout our lives, we'll run into problems, because our irrational beliefs make us think we should achieve impossible things.

> *"Reality is not so much what happens to us; rather, it is how we think about those events that create the reality we experience. In a very real sense, this means that we each create the reality in which we live."*
> Albert Ellis

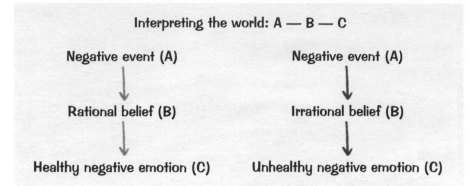

Interpreting the world: A — B — C

Negative event (A)	Negative event (A)
↓	↓
Rational belief (B)	Irrational belief (B)
↓	↓
Healthy negative emotion (C)	Unhealthy negative emotion (C)

Ellis developed the ABC method, which shows the ways that we contribute to making ourselves feel upset, sad or "bad." "A" stands for Activating event, "B" for Belief and "C" for Consequence.

For instance, some people think that they should be thoroughly competent at everything, regardless of their intelligence level or aptitude for various tasks. Or they may think that they need someone stronger to depend upon. Others believe there is a perfect solution to all human problems, if only they could find it. Ellis would encourage his clients to question these assumptions. Does every problem really have a perfect solution? And even if there is one, is there any reason why that particular solution should ever be found?

Misinterpretation

It's the way that we think about and interpret situations that causes us difficulty, according to Ellis, not the situations themselves. Just as we can't make everyone else like us, no one can make us feel a particular emotion either. In response to your partner calling you "an idiot," you might say that she or he "made me angry," but this is not the case, said Ellis. For this to be true, it would always have to be the case that, when X does Y, the resulting

emotion is Z. But some people would allow that comment to sail over their heads, while others might laugh and still others wonder what's got into that person today. It's the distorted beliefs we're running that send us off down perilous paths of overthinking, and we need to get a hold of them as soon as possible and sort them out. In technical terms, we need to identify and challenge such thinking, rephrase the problem in a way that more accurately reflects reality, and adopt strategies that will change assumptions into healthier, evidence-based thinking.

In his 1975 book, *A New Guide to Rational Living,* written with Robert Harper, Ellis identified 10 typical irrational beliefs and put together the "disputing statements" with which we need to counter them. Luckily, Irrational Idea No. 1 is exactly the one we need for the common idea that "you must — yes, must — have love or approval from all the people you find significant." Most people enjoy approval, Ellis said, and so it's good to have it, but you won't die if you don't have it. On the other hand, you may harm yourself by pursuing the impossible ideal of having everyone love you, which is why it's essential to reshape this belief as soon as possible.

The rational answer

Ellis' reasoning on this point goes something like this. It's impossible to be liked or loved by everybody. No matter how popular you are, there will always be someone who doesn't like you, and that's fine. Different people have different tastes, so some people will like things about you that others dislike, such as your hairstyle — it's impossible for everyone to agree that long hair with a center parting is the only way to go. Even if you could get everybody to like or love you, you would never know if they liked you enough, or if they continued to like you. Where's the point at which you say "Yes! I succeeded"?

There's no harm in trying to be popular, in a relaxed kind of way, but it's best not to try too hard, according to Ellis. It's self-helping to want to be popular, but it's self-defeating to need to be popular. The attempt could exhaust you, with all the time and effort you'd feel compelled to put in, leaving you no time for the things you want to do. And if you're trying to fulfill their ideas of the right way to look, or the perfect holidays to take, you'll always be doing what your friends want you to do, not what you want to do. Your life will no longer be your own, and your efforts could even backfire — your friends might end up seeing you as a sycophant and lose respect for you.

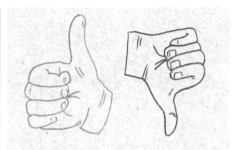

It's impossible for everyone to like us, says Ellis, so we need to accept that we'll always produce a mixed response in other people.

Argue with yourself if you feel upset that someone's unfriended you, Ellis would say. Take it as a sign of individuality and a step on the route toward self-acceptance and self-approval, which is much surer ground than the approval of others. Live your own life, do your own thing, and you'll find a few true and interesting friends along the way without even trying. (I bow to the king of disputation, because I wouldn't argue with that.)

Key theories

Rational Emotive Behavioral Therapy
—Albert Ellis

Why is my boss always so mean?

Carl Jung • Wilfred Bion • Harold J. Leavitt • René Girard

Bullying in the workplace is rampant — surveys in the United States and the UK consistently find that around 33 percent of workers have been on the receiving end of bullying behavior. The International Labour Organization (ILO) suggests that the risk of physical and emotional violence is one of the most serious problems organizations will face over the next millennium. That's a pretty big claim, and means that if your boss is mean you're not only not alone, but part of a disturbing trend in firms around the global marketplace. The psychoanalyst Carl Jung would see this global reach as a manifestation of the "collective unconscious" and suggest that perhaps the Shadow is in play.

Jung saw each of us as having both conscious and unconscious parts to our personalities, and believed that the unconscious is made up of various personified structures that interact with each other in our inner world. These structures became known as the *archetypes* (see page 136), and they are frameworks for approaching the external world. In common speech, an archetype is the first mold or model of something, which later versions refer back to in some way, and Jung's use of the term is not dissimilar. He held that the human mind has access to ideas of characters — such as the hero or the evil stepmother — that help us interpret and understand the world, and determine what actions to take. The reason these characters or archetypes turn up in fairy tales, myths and even religions all around the world, he said, is because they are held in the collective unconscious; they are "deposits of the constantly repeated experiences of humanity."

This suggests that certain types of people and ways of being have always been around, and having made it into the collective unconscious, the ideas of them (the archetypes) are passed on to the mind of every generation, allowing us to recognize them at play in other people, but also in ourselves. Two of the most important are the Persona and its counterpart, the Shadow. The Persona is a mask we put on

> *"Everyone carries a Shadow, and the less it is embodied in the individual's life, the blacker and denser it is."*
> Carl Jung

Five neurotic modes of dysfunctional organizations that can lead to the development of scapegoating dynamics:

1

Paranoid organizations
These firms constantly fear being targeted by threats that may affect their functioning. Every problem or potential threat is analyzed by considering all possible elements, even when this is extremely costly or time-consuming.

2

Obsessive organizations
Management controls in these firms are designed to closely monitor internal business, production efficiency, costs, etc. Rely highly on tradition and consolidated practices.

3

Hysterical organizations
Unable to adapt their structure to new operational needs, these firms are hyperactive and impulsive, and led by the values and ideas of their CEO rather than responding to external events.

4

Depressive organizations
These are very bureaucratic firms that function automatically with little or no leadership, seeming to drift along. Their main features are inactivity, lack of trust and extreme conservatism.

5

Schizoid organizations
These firms lack true leadership: the leader appears to have no interest in the organization, refuses to be consistent, and won't listen to others, so the company zigzags back and forth in direction according to continual influx of new management.

Displacing the blame

Girard suggests that when conflict causes a group to fragment, its members often seek reconciliation through choosing a victim to scapegoat. This person is then denounced "with great fervour and sincerity" before being expelled from the group. It is usually obvious to people outside the group that the victim is not really responsible for the "crime" of which they are accused.

to present ourselves in the world; it's the image we wish to present to other people, but also to ourselves. Freud and Jung agreed that all of us are happy to acknowledge our "good parts" but less keen to admit to those we see as "bad" or shameful in some way.

Enter the Shadow

Jung suggested that all these "bad" parts are coalesced into the internal archetype of the Shadow; this is the dark side of our personalities that holds every trait we have ever disowned. The Shadow is necessarily hidden and repressed, even from ourselves, and because it's made up of traits that we think are unforgivable, there's a fair amount of guilt, shame and inferiority attached. Unfortunately, although we try desperately hard to keep it so under wraps so that we can pretend it's not there, it will out, especially under conditions of stress. The Shadow is the part of us that erupts

spontaneously and unexpectedly when we do something hurtful to ourselves or another person, and afterward say, "I can't believe I just did that!" If in doubt, you'll recognize it by its calling card: the feeling of guilt, humiliation and shame that follows a sudden Shadow outburst.

Jumping shadows

Very often the Shadow appears in someone else — or at least that's what seems to be happening. The psychoanalytic defense known as "projection" is a way in which we deny an unpleasant feeling in ourselves by seeing it instead in someone else: we project it onto them. The Shadow often appears in projection. For instance, if someone in a position of power lets rip at an employee about their extreme lack of usefulness or skills, it's entirely possible that they themselves are feeling useless and, unable to bear this feeling, are throwing it across the room onto someone else. Then

> *"All peoples have a tendency to reject, under some pretext or another, the individuals who don't fit their conception of what is normal and acceptable."*
> René Girard

they feel much better, even though they are unaware of their unconscious motivation.

So it's possible that your boss' spitefulness owes much to his or her sense of inadequacy, which they find impossible to countenance. The Shadow may erupt only occasionally ("she's not herself today") or threaten to push the Ego out of the way and even swap sides with it, so that the Shadow becomes the dominant everyday part.

Why me?

One of the most commonly held beliefs about bullying is that the victim invites vindictive behavior in some way, and there is evidence that people who were brought up in very authoritarian types of households gravitate toward relationships that echo this uneven power dynamic.

There is, however, another, quite different, potential "victim" — someone who feels a greater need for independence than for affiliation. Someone, in other words, who won't conform to group values, ideals or goals just because these are currently held by the group, but seeks instead to maintain an independent line of thought and way of being.

This independence, according to psychoanalyst **Wilfred Bion**, is experienced as threatening by other group members. The group's values have been put in place by an authoritative leader (not unlike the authoritarian head of a family) who

"knows what's best" for the firm and has been at pains to convey these ideas to the workforce and to impose them on it. According to managerial psychologist **Harold J. Leavitt** every group has a drive toward conformism and an acceptance of how the group should think, behave, act and value. These are "centripetal forces" that bring about common identity and a sense of unity. Everything is known and understood. Everything is safe and predictable — until, that is, someone arrives who begins to question things. Why are we using this outdated software instead of that newer, much better one? Why aren't we hot-ly looking for greater efficiency? Let's shake things up a bit!

"Let's not" is the instinctive response of the group. And like hearing a siren going off on an ocean cruiser, everyone starts rushing around in a panic (their jobs and identities feel threatened, their work functions seem suddenly unclear). Something must be done! And the solution is … throw the new person overboard! Get rid of the problem, fast!

This phenomenon has become known as "scapegoating" and it has been examined in detail by French social scientist **René Girard**, who suggested that the entire process happens beneath the level of awareness, even while being played out. The way it works is that undue blame is placed on someone during a period of crisis (which might be real or only perceived),

> *"The shadow belongs to the wholeness of the personality: the strong man must somewhere be weak, somewhere the clever man must be stupid, otherwise he is too good to be true and falls back on pose and bluff."*
> Carl Jung

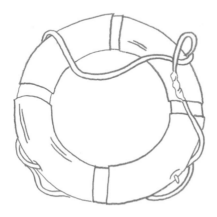

so that the person becomes the target and center of escalating hostility. The goal of scapegoating is the ultimate expulsion of the target ("Let's just get rid of that person — then we'll be fine.").

Another way of seeing the scapegoating process is in terms of the Shadow, which can operate at a personal and also at a collective level. In the collective form, it occurs in the shape of a group, which may be anything from a small niche group to an entire company or even a political party or government. The group projects its collective Shadow, such as economic failure, onto a convenient scapegoat — which might be an individual or another group (such as immigrants or a religious group). Victims might seek recourse to reality, by whistleblowing or leaking stories to the media, but this won't

work, according to Jung, because there is no escape from the Shadow. Someone has to carry this dark stuff that the individual or the group doesn't want, and it's going to be … you.

So if you're an independent soul who feels out of step with the organization, and notice that you are becoming the target of the boss' minions, or even your whole department, it may be worth using one of the lifeboats before they throw you off the deck. If it's any comfort, the relief from expelling a scapegoat is short-lived, and another will soon need to be found. At the same time, it's possible that your own Shadow includes the need always to be an outsider, and never belong. And if that feels absolutely impossible, it's probably true.

Key theories
The **Shadow archetype**
— Carl Jung
Group dynamics
— Wilfred Bion
Scapegoating — René Girard

My family's a nightmare — shall I cut them off?

Murray Bowen

As adults, we tend to feel that our psyches are complete and our own, and that we are moving around the world making free choices with rational minds. All of those assumptions have now been questioned by psychologists and neuroscientists, but they were still intact until World War II, when returning veterans threw up a new problem for psychiatrists: why did their psychological issues get worse when they returned home to their families? It seems that you are experiencing a similar kind of problem. Why do our families continue to affect us so much?

The 1940s saw the birth of a new idea in therapy: that we are not born with fixed temperaments so much as molded through the relationships we have with other people. This idea became the focus of the work of psychiatrist Murray Bowen, who began to shift from an individual focus on patients to an understanding of whole families as "human emotional systems." He worked in many cases with schizophrenics, but his family work made him realize that there is something of a continuum in play; families differ quantitatively but not qualitatively, he said, noting that "there is a little schizophrenia in all of us."

Woven into a matrix

By this Bowen meant that it's the way we function around one another that contributes to the development of emotional health or disorders (such as schizophrenia) in others. We continually do things that help or hinder other people and affect their functioning in the world; we pass judgments, make emotional demands on them or refuse to acknowledge their emotional needs. We hear and see them, and let them know this, or we don't hear or see them, and we reflect this instead. We expect things from them, especially certain types of behavior, and we are disappointed or angry when these fail to materialize. And we do all of these things in a more extreme and intense way within our families, parents most of all.

The emotional intensity of the connection among family members increases the level of effect on one another, particularly in the way that parents reaffirm or challenge a child's reality and sense of importance (presence, even) in the world, in ways that help them develop well-defined, independent selves or, alternatively, less defined, more dependent selves who continually seek acknowledgment and approval from others. Those with a strong differentiation of self are able to separate thoughts and feelings, to respond in a skillful way to anxiety and to maintain their

The four questions to ask while trying to individuate ("grow away" from) family roles and systems

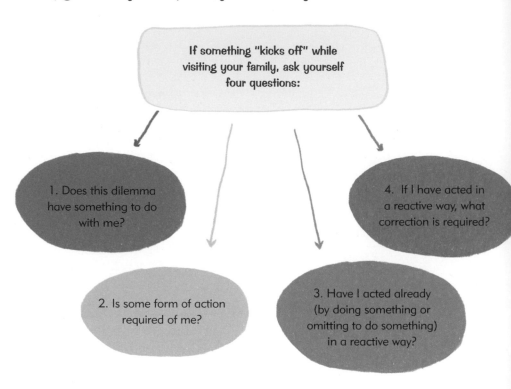

If something "kicks off" while visiting your family, ask yourself four questions:

1. Does this dilemma have something to do with me?

2. Is some form of action required of me?

3. Have I acted already (by doing something or omitting to do something) in a reactive way?

4. If I have acted in a reactive way, what correction is required?

individuality even within the family group. People with a lower level of differentiation tend to experience a kind of "emotional fusion" within the family, feeling what the group feels, anticipating its members' needs and acting in ways that help to keep the system in balance. They have diffuse boundaries and are acting in the group's interest, not their own. In a sense, they lose themselves within the group.

Strength in cohesion

Bowen said that, in evolutionary terms, families developed to protect, shelter and feed their members and, to do this, each family group needs cohesiveness and cooperation. We're all working together, right? However, the rules and demands are not explicitly stated: members work out what's needed from them to keep everyone

> *"Differentiation is charting one's own way by means of one's own internal guidance system, rather than perpetually eyeing the 'scope' to see where others are at."*
> Edwin Friedman

happy. This means that cohesiveness is often gained in ways that hinder the true differentiation of each family member, and require some of them to take on roles that are uncomfortable and ultimately destructive. For instance, in families where one of the parents is an alcoholic, the other parent may be taken up with taking care of everything thrown up by the alcoholic's behavior, so the children pick up the slack in terms of parenting. One child may become the main caretaker, another the joker, another the one to hold all the sadness in the family so no one else has to feel it, and so on.

Cutting off to escape

Bowen identified a common way that we use to get away from our uncomfortable, outdated family roles without dealing with them, which he called "emotional cutoff." We think that if we create a distance between ourselves and other family members, we'll be free of the ways we find ourselves feeling and acting around them. Bowen, however, says that this technique doesn't work. The roles we take on in childhood to maintain the ongoing family system stay with us, because they're part of us, even though they developed within a system (the family). If these roles are not exercised in the original family system, because we've cut off members of our family, they will begin to emerge in a newer relationship, following

a brief honeymoon period of all seemingly being well. While the cutoff might bring a feeling of immediate relief and escape, our patterns of reactivity within any kind of relationship remain unchanged and will keep repeating. This is why in newer relationships we often find ourselves thinking, "Oh, no, not this again!"

On the other hand, when someone vows to go back to the family after a cutoff period, all hell tends to break loose, because the feelings that drove that person away are still boiling under the surface. Old interactions surface within hours, resulting in icy politeness and tremendous undercurrents, or shouting matches, crying and hysterics. For instance, you may have decided to cut off family members because you were sick of being blamed for everything, only to find your parents becoming increasingly anxious and your siblings seeking to defuse the mounting tension by insisting that you leave. This is because the family members are now trying to rebalance the family system — like a very delicate mobile in a gust of wind — by cutting *you* off. The system is in the process of rebalancing without you.

So should I go home or stay away?

Bowen draws a distinction between "breaking away" and "growing away," and it's the latter that holds the possibility of positive change. This is a way of achieving

> *"It is only when one can get a little outside of one's patterned ways of responding (and the accompanying inner intellectual and emotional fusion) that it is possible to begin to observe."*
> Murray Bowen

System in balance

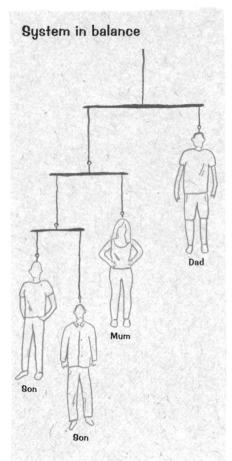

Dad

Mum

Son

Son

Bowen said that families work as systems, with each family member playing a role that allows the family to function, even if only dysfunctionally.

independence, not just distance, through the identification and following of our own, independent goals while still recognizing that we are part of the family system. Through identifying our family roles, relational patterns and the ways in which we contribute to those patterns, we can dissolve them and ultimately find ourselves in the much stronger position of freely choosing our responses within all forms of relationship.

As with so many emotional challenges, change begins with coming off autopilot long enough to catch yourself reacting and noticing what's happening right here and now, in yourself, rather than the rest of your family. They're so distracting though, aren't they? That crazy dance still has some unfathomable kind of appeal. It may be hard to drag your eyes from their whirling feet to look at your own. But keep watching. They'll soon start tapping to a new tune.

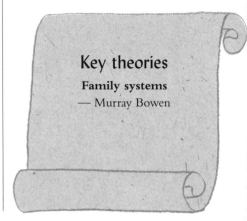

Key theories

Family systems
— Murray Bowen

Is my partner lying to me?

Sigmund Freud • Paul Ekman

We all lie, so the easy answer is, "Yes, probably," because studies have found that, on average, adults lie 13 times a week. But there seems to be another query behind your question, which has something to do with morality. If he or she is deceiving you about something, is this automatically wrong? It may not be wise for me to get into a discussion of lying and immorality, because even psychologists use deceptive techniques for experimental reasons, with the justification, presumably, that the end justifies the means. On the other hand, we teach our children that lying is wrong and tell them not to do it; we might even accompany this with some form of threatened punishment that we have absolutely no intention of carrying out — therefore lying to ourselves in the process.

Of course we're all going to lie. It's a part of being human. In fact, it's seen as a milestone in human development because very young children see their parents as impossibly perfect — all-seeing, all-knowing and all-powerful, until one day the scales drop from their eyes. They test their parent with a small falsehood, only to discover that mom or dad believes them and takes their story as fact. They don't know everything! This is great and thrilling news for the child, aged around 2, because it gives her a newfound sense of independence. In **Freud**ian or psychoanalytic terms, lying is up there with two other milestones — saying, "No!" and being able to play hide-and-seek without shouting out where you're hiding. This is because all three of these acts evidence the wonderful fact that parents can't read our minds, which as infants we assumed they could.

Lying as fantasy

This is very liberating, but it's possible to get carried away. Psychologist Bryan King reports seeing a client who claimed to have spoken a sentence at 3 months old, given a sermon at church aged just 3 years, and worked at a magazine that paid him $8 million a week. This creative soul was suffering from *pseudologia fantastica*, or pathological lying, which knows no bounds

> "The stronger the emotion, the more likely it is that some sign of it will leak despite the liar's best attempt to conceal it."
> Paul Ekman

Micro expressions

Fear
Eyebrows raised and drawn together • Forehead wrinkles between the brows • Upper eyelid raised; lower lid tense and drawn up • Upper white of eye showing • Mouth open and lips drawn back

Disgust
Upper eyelid, lower lip and cheeks raised • Nose wrinkled • Lines show below the lower eyelid.

Anger
Brows lowered and drawn together • Lower eyelid tensed • Eyes staring or bulging • Lips pursed together with corners down • Nostrils dilated • Lower jaw jutting out

Contempt
One side of mouth raises

in its confabulations and often produces self-aggrandizing statements well beyond the limits that might keep the listener in doubt. This is lying without a care for being believed, but it is still difficult to diagnose, because the level of lying can fluctuate and the diagnosis depends mainly on self-reporting, which is clearly somewhat unreliable in this case.

Inner and outer worlds

So lying is sometimes good and sometimes healthy, but persistent lying is seen by psychoanalysts as damaging — lies damage trust, cut us off from other people, cause us stress (especially when they begin to string together), make us oversensitive and ultimately affect our capacity to think truthfully. In extreme cases lying can distort our ability to recognize reality, because it breaks down the communication between our inner and outer worlds in some way. We tend to forget that, all the time we're awake and conscious, we're interpreting the external world with our minds — representing the outer world in our inner world. This happens automatically, so we don't generally need to think about it, but when we lie, we deliberately break this link in some way. This is why professional con artists and hustlers advise would-be liars to believe their made-up stories, thus bringing the inner and outer worlds back into alignment. Except this time neither of them is reflecting reality.

If you really want to know whether your partner is lying, it's the idea of congruence that may be of most help. In the same way

that lying creates a mismatch between the facts of the external world and the way we're representing it in our heads, the same mismatch will be apparent in the way that we re-present our internal story back to the external world — that's to say, when we come out with the lie.

Our faces give us away

The world's leading expert on lying is psychologist **Paul Ekman**, whose work has focused on emotions and their relation to facial expressions; in other words, the external ways in which we betray our innermost thoughts and feelings. His research work among isolated communities convinced him that Charles Darwin was right: facial expressions are universal and not learned. He went on to design a *Facial Action Coding System* to measure facial expressions through the activity of the muscles beneath them, leading him to be able to detect the tiniest, quickest, involuntary flashes of emotion, or "micro expressions," which give away the truth of the inner world in a quarter of a second, no matter how hard a person tries to disguise them. From the U.S. and UK to Papua New Guinea, Japan, Brazil and beyond, seven emotions — disgust, anger, fear, sadness, surprise, contempt and happiness — are always displayed using the same facial muscles. This information has proved invaluable to police, antiterrorist and government forces around the world. So it may be useful to you, as you drum your fingers on your lap and wonder about the truth of your partner's words.

> *"Microexpressions, the very fast signs of concealed emotion that occur in ¹⁄₂₅ of a second, never lie."*
> Paul Ekman

Ekman says that there is no silver bullet for detecting when someone is lying, and that even a polygraph (the so-called "lie detector") performs little better than random chance. It can indicate unease or a hidden emotion, but this may be due to nervousness about not being believed, rather than indicating lying, so it is far from infallible. Fidgeting — long thought to be a sign of lying, especially by schoolteachers, it seems — is simply a sign of unease and not necessarily of lying.

Signs of lying

However, Ekman does claim that there are certain "hot spots" or conflicts between words spoken and physical gestures that indicate that you're not getting the full, truthful story. Micro-facial expressions such as fear, disgust, anger or contempt might give you an idea of the feelings behind someone's words (*see* illustration, page 120), and indicate concealed emotions. Likewise, signs of incongruence, such as a slight head shake from side to side (saying, "No") while the person is verbally saying, "Yes," or a small shrug of one shoulder while verbally announcing confidence about themselves or a fact. Many signs may be useful in building up the larger picture: the words, the voice, posture, gaze, and gestures large and small. Increased blinking, for example, is a sign of someone having to think harder and, while liars have been found to have a slow blink rate, this changes in certain circumstances. For instance, if someone is

lying about a transgression that makes them feel anxious, the anxiety would raise their blink level. Dilated pupils are another sign of concentration, and so may betray lying or anxiety.

Liars avoid eye contact when they're highly motivated not to get caught, so watch your partner's eyes if you want to check out a possible lie. If his or her eyes lock onto yours while denying something, it means they may be lying, but they're not anxious about issuing a denial. It means they don't care what you think. This might give you pause. Are you sure you want to go there? "Most of us want to put off bad news," says Ekman, because "the truth can be painful." We may choose to avoid it even when we are picking up signals that something is wrong. So, it may not be your partner lying that's the problem, so much as your fear of facing the truth. Now we're back in Freudian territory. Once more onto the couch, dear reader?

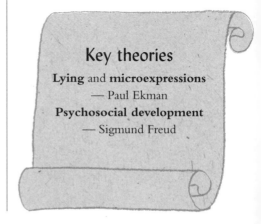

Key theories
Lying and **microexpressions**
— Paul Ekman
Psychosocial development
— Sigmund Freud

My boss is so cool — she's quick, articulate, organized and even well dressed. Why aren't I like that?

Melanie Klein • Ronald Fairbairn

It sounds as though your boss is perfect...which, of course, is impossible. Being human, she will be making mistakes all over the place, just like the rest of us. But it seems you don't see those mistakes, so something is clouding your vision. Psychoanalysts describe this as a process of idealization, stemming from a choice you made long ago: "Is she the bad one, or am I?"

In the 1920s a new branch of psychoanalysis called *Object Relations Theory* began to develop. Freud had used the word "object" to denote the target of our inner drives but he hadn't paid it much attention, because his theory of primary narcissism meant that he saw all the energies and drives of early development as directed toward the self. However, one of Freud's disciples named **Melanie Klein** began working with children, and she suggested that other people — external "objects" — are hugely important to the formation of self and the way we view the world, other people and ourselves. What's more, the processes we use then and the conclusions we come to will dictate our relationships with other people for the rest of our lives. Suddenly, "relationship" moved center stage in psychoanalysis, where it has remained ever since. In the process, analysts realized why some of us have a tendency to see the world in black and white, positioning other people as wholly bad or wholly good ("perfect" in fact).

Inner and outer worlds

Klein hypothesized that infants suffer an almost overwhelming amount of anxiety, from an internal "death instinct" that threatens to kill them, the trauma of the birth itself and early experiences of hunger and frustration. Infants also have an intensely fertile imagination, she said, and have fantasies about all sorts of things, as well as a built-in tendency to make internal representations of everything they come into contact with. They are constantly internalizing "objects" (such as parents), making mental representations of them, mixing these with their own fantasies and anxieties, and then projecting the mental representation back onto the people in the external world — which means they now see these people in this new, adjusted way.

This is quite a feat by the baby, so how does it happen? Klein says that the infant takes her good and bad feelings and projects them onto objects in the world, and the first things she encounters of real importance

123

are her mother's breasts. It is onto these the baby projects both her loving and hating feelings. The "good breast" is the mother who is now seen as loving and loved; she holds all the baby's projection of the libido, or life instinct. The "bad breast" is the mother who is perceived as persecutory and hating, and on whom the baby can project all her "bad" feelings. Over time, the child begins to bring these two mothers into one, by a cyclical process of continually internalizing and projecting representations that gradually allows more of the real mother into the mentalized versions, until they form one merged "object" that contains both good and bad elements. This is Donald Winnicott's "good enough" mother (see page 78).

This joining together of the good and bad mothers is essential for healthy development, according to Klein, because it also helps the baby begin to integrate the different parts of herself, so that she does not see herself as entirely "good" or "bad." In addition, it's how we learn that people may react along a continuum of helpful or harmful behavior; instead of seeing people as absolutely perfect (idealizing them) or absolutely bad (denigrating them), we realize that one person can encompass many moods and types of behavior.

Less fantasy, more reality

Klein insisted that the child's inner anxiety controls the way that objects are perceived, but in the 1940s the psychoanalyst **Ronald Fairbairn** swung the focus away from the child's inner world and more toward the realities of the external world. He said that the baby has two different representations of the mother because the mother really does have different moods and approaches to the baby — it's not just projection. However, if the mother responds in a sensitive and attuned way to the baby's needs most of the time, the child's anxiety begins to ease, and she is able

"It is difficult to imagine any person with an ego so unified and stable at its higher levels that in no circumstances whatever would any evidence of basic splitting come to the surface."
Ronald Fairbairn

> *"The aim of psychoanalytic treatment is to effect breaches of the closed system which constitutes the patient's inner world, and thus to make this world accessible to the influence of outer reality."*
> Ronald Fairbairn

to integrate the two internal representations (good mom/bad mom) into one "good enough" mother, as Klein suggested.

A parent must be seen as good

The real problem though, says Fairbairn, is what happens if the baby is cared for by an emotionally absent, intrusive, inconsistent or chaotic parent. This feels both painful and dangerous to the child, who depends on his caregivers for the sustenance of life. In this scenario, the only way to feel safe is to repress the idea of the bad parent completely to effectively "make the bad mom go away." However, this leaves a problem: if the mother is all-good, why is she not responding to his cries for food or help? There must be some reason … Ah! The baby realizes that it must be because he is bad; if he were good, the all-good parent would look after him. In this moment, the infant takes all the "badness" that belonged to the repressed mother image and puts it firmly onto himself. By doing this, he absorbs all the parent's depression, disorganization or sadism ("badness"), obtaining external security by sacrificing his inner security. As Fairbairn explains, it feels "better to live as a sinner in a world ruled by God than to live in a world ruled by the devil." He called this *The Moral Defense*. But something terrible has happened: the feeling of "badness" will

always, now, rest within that child, and the "goodness" will always be seen to rest in someone else.

This is a truly tragic position, because although it originated in the pattern of relationship between parent and child, psychoanalysts believe it then plays out within all the other relationships of that person's life. The "splitting" of an "other" into all-good and all-bad originated in anxiety, so it may arise again as a defense when an individual is unable to integrate difficult feelings, particularly when feeling anxious around someone perceived as being in an authoritative position. By idealizing that person — such as your boss — you no longer need to worry; she'll take care of everything in a supremely competent

125

> *"The bad object is denied, as is the whole situation of frustration and the bad feelings (pain) to which frustration gives rise."*
> Melanie Klein

way, because she can do anything! She's the all-good parent and you just need to try harder. You feel recognized, understood and completely safe, but you don't really know why. This is because the inner call for the splitting and projective defense has been done unconsciously in the replay of that original relationship. You experience the result of the defense, wihout noticing it kick in.

Crashing out

Unfortunately this feel-good moment won't last long, because the flip side of idealization is *devaluation*. You have placed your boss on the highest of pedestals (the all-good parent), and the inevitable fall will be immense. As she falls, she will transform from being the beautiful, perfect object of your affection and admiration into a fallible, broken thing. At this point, the scales drop from your eyes — now she looks like an idiot! How could you have been so dense?

There's no possibility of integration for someone who didn't learn how to bring together good mom/bad mom as a child, so people are seen as either completely wonderful or complete disappointments. This is the core of black-and-white thinking, underwritten by an occasional flash of inadequacy ("How could I have been so dense?") that must be defended against immediately by a new idealization ("I've just got the most amazing personal trainer!").

It's exhausting, all this putting of people on pedestals and then ripping them down. Although it feels good in the idealization stage, the downs of the devaluations are painful and confusing. They are ripples of the same disappointment of the parent's early failings and they can feel just as crushing. And yet it is in the disappointment that true hope can be found. As the self-deluding hope of a rescuing, all-powerful Other crashes to the ground, you may get a glimpse of what it was you really wanted, but didn't believe yourself capable of achieving. It's all your own goodness up for grabs. In the fall of the idol, the magic of idealization gives way to reality, just briefly — it's almost within your grasp — before you push it away again as impossible, and return to a place of useless desolation, handing all your power into the hands of a new Other. Unless … once more onto the couch, dear reader?

Key theories

Splitting
— Melanie Klein
The moral defense
— Ronald Fairbairn

"The ego is incapable of splitting the object... without a corresponding splitting taking place within the ego."

What's happening?

Page 130: Why do I keep saying embarrassing things?

Page 134: What's the real appeal of *Harry Potter*?

Page 141: I wish I hadn't sold that house.

Page 146: Should I work for love or money?

Page 150: Why do I always buy the more expensive option?

Page 154: What's the point?

Chapter 4

Why do I keep saying embarrassing things?

Sigmund Freud • Donald Norman • James Reason

"I'd like to spank all the teachers …" Thus spake President George W. Bush to a national teachers' conference when he wished, apparently sincerely, to thank them for all their hard work. Awkward? Very. Indication of a secret desire? That's up for grabs. Freud insisted that these kinds of word slips, or "Freudian slips" as they became known, reveal a truth that the speaker wishes to conceal, perhaps even from themselves. Freud would say *especially* from themselves, because it reveals a deeply held belief that they'd rather deny. Nonsense, say the psychologists — cognitive psychology can suggest much simpler reasons for word slips and lapses of memory, so they mean nothing at all. So what's really going on?

In 1901 **Freud** wrote a book examining the psychopathology of everyday life, handily titled with those very words. This was not an examination of the habits of people suffering from an unusual state of mind, but of all of us, every day. Freud was fascinated by these commonplace oddities because he saw them, like dreams, as evidence of the existence of the unconscious and its operations. The "wrong" word is not random but meaningful, he said, and tracing its meaning can prove enlightening for the speaker. He claimed that they also show "that the borderline between the normal and the abnormal in nervous matters is a fluid one, and that we are all a little neurotic."

That's certainly a leveling idea, if a little uncomfortable for most of us. So thank goodness that today's cognitive psychologists insist that slips reveal no more than straightforward mechanics of the mind.

Psychologist **Donald Norman**, who has studied these slips in detail, claims that the most common forms of slip occur because of the intrusion of habit. He suggests the example of standing at a friend's door trying to unlock it with your own house key. It's hard not to see Freud falling on that example with delight, but Dr. Norman says that it's simply a matter of using a habitual sequence that is easily recognizable as linked to some activity that is more frequent, recent or familiar than the one in hand.

Meaningless error

Essentially, Norman says, slips of speech or action require some kind of cognitive "under-specification," like inattention, incomplete sense data or insufficient knowledge, and the existence of a response pattern that's appropriate to the situation.

Psychologist **James Reason** suggests that, in addition, people who are prone to one kind of mistake, such as a slip of the tongue, are equally prone to other kinds of slips, such as behavioral ones. He concludes that what we're looking at here is some kind of general factor exerting influence across all aspects of mental function, and that factor is a failure to suppress competing choices.

Dr. Reason (who has the most glorious name for a cognitive psychologist) is saying that when the mind fails to suppress an alternative to the one required, a slip occurs. Precisely, Freud would argue! Suppression is the key. And what is causing the lack of suppression of this particular "wrong" word? Dr. Reason might suggest a *cognitive confusion* of words that sound the same, at least in part, but Freud would pounce on this immediately. "It is instant shame!" he would announce. Shame and guilt over a desire or thought that conflicts with the way we like to think about ourselves.

Freud foresaw the potential arguments against his explanation of verbal slips and said that things like absentmindedness, distraction, excitement, exhaustion or intoxication are in the mix, but on their own they don't offer enough of an explanation. They "facilitate the slip by pointing out a path for it to take. But if there is a path before me, does it necessarily follow that I must go along it? I also require a motive determining my choice, some force to propel me forward."

We delight in obvious slips that seem instantly to betray the speaker's real feelings, such as the swollen-headedness behind UK Prime Minister Gordon Brown's

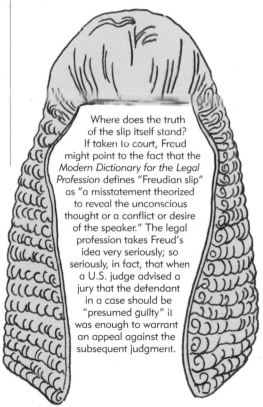

Where does the truth of the slip itself stand? If taken to court, Freud might point to the fact that the *Modern Dictionary for the Legal Profession* defines "Freudian slip" as "a misstatement theorized to reveal the unconscious thought or a conflict or desire of the speaker." The legal profession takes Freud's idea very seriously; so seriously, in fact, that when a U.S. judge advised a jury that the defendant in a case should be "presumed guilty" it was enough to warrant an appeal against the subsequent judgment.

Famous Freudian slips

> "Rarely is the question asked: Is our children learning?"

George W. Bush, U.S. President and firm believer in the education system, during a speech in 2000.

> "Work is the curse of the drinking classes."

Reverend William A. Spooner, who had meant to say "Drink is the curse of the working classes," became renowned for his slips, so much so that the word "spoonerism" was coined to describe such a speech error.

> "Weapons of Mass Distraction"

Australian Prime Minister Kevin Rudd referring to chemical weapons during a press conference in 2013. He swiftly corrected himself.

> "This president is going to lead us out of this recovery."

Dan Quayle (ex U.S. Vice President) during a campaign stop in 1992.

announcement in December 2008 to the UK Parliament that, "We not only saved the world, er, saved the banks ..." or the later Prime Minister David Cameron's self-defeating claim that he was "raising more money for the rich" when trying to insist that his forthcoming tax reforms would help the poor. Or Kim Kardashian's husband, Kanye West, tweeting, "Up early in the morning taking meetings in Silicone Valley," later corrected to "Silicon" to establish that he wasn't referring to the material used in cosmetic surgery. Even President Obama fell prey to the odd slip, such as this one, which gives us cause to wonder how he saw life beyond the White House: "We should

be reforming our criminal justice system in such a way that we are not incarcerating nonviolent offenders in ways that renders them incapable of getting a job after they leave office" (rather than jail).

On the couch

Freud's approach to the phenomenon was more nuanced than ours as he tracked down the meaning behind slips that cropped up in his patients' speech in terms of complexes, but also, at times, in terms of simple desire or fear. He describes one young doctor timidly and reverently introducing himself to the celebrated Dr. Virchow with the following words: "I am Dr. Virchow." The surprised professor turned to the young man and asked, "Is your name also Virchow?" Freud wonders whether the young man felt so insignificant next to this "big man" that his own name escaped him, and also whether the young man had the courage to admit that he secretly hoped to one day be as great a man as the professor.

Another patient, keen to show that he was not a representative member of the "useless generation" he perceived around him, used a Latin proverb but omitted one word: *aliquis* (meaning someone). He challenged Freud to analyze the slip, so Freud began by asking the man to tell him "candidly and uncritically, whatever comes into your mind if you direct your attention to the forgotten word." The man begins to produce a sequence of associations: *aliquis*, a–liquis, *reliquiae* (relics), liquefying, fluidity, fluid, Simon of Trent, the accusation against the Jews of ritual blood sacrifice … new editions of the Savior … an article about St. Augustine on Women … St. Benedict, St. Augustine, St. Januarius — the saint who performed "the miracle of the blood." He explains how the blood of St. Januarius is said to *liquify* on a particular holy day. He begins to speak about the miracle of the blood again but stops mid-sentence; when prompted by Freud he reveals his concern about a young woman who might soon be revealing some "awkward news." "That her periods have stopped?" asks Freud. "How could you guess that?" the young man responds in some consternation.

Why does it matter?

Freud claims that slips (such as you find yourself making) reveal a conflict between something that insists on being said and an inner force that seeks to repress it. Interestingly, there's also a conflict between the popular espousal of the idea of Freudian slips (they circulate endlessly online to our amusement) and modern psychology's reluctance to accept them as anything more than an innocent case of mistaken speech. In essence, this is really a battle over the existence of the unconscious itself; if slips are nothing but clumsy and meaningless "mistakes" of the mind, there is no reason to assume the unconscious's existence. If they hold meaning, however, then it seems that something beyond the rational conscious mind has momentarily made itself known. It is the idea of the unconscious itself that the psychologists wish to formally repress. And no one would appreciate the irony of that more than Dr. Freud.

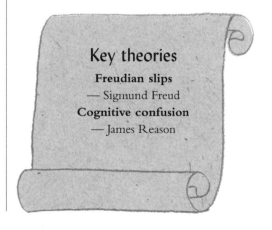

Key theories

Freudian slips
— Sigmund Freud
Cognitive confusion
— James Reason

What's the real appeal of *Harry Potter?*

Carl Jung • Donald Kalsched • Donald Winnicott

There are now more than 450 million copies of *Harry Potter* books in print across 73 different languages, and the series continues to sell to children and adults around the world, seemingly regardless of culture or background. So what is it about the books that appeals to millions of people? The answer may lie in the mythopoetic level of mind that Carl Jung said exists in all of us, which is peopled by magical archetypes that have the power to save us in the real world.

As with all stories, we need to start at the beginning, with *Harry Potter and the Philosopher's Stone* (published in the United States as *Harry Potter and the Sorcerer's Stone*) The stone in question is a legendary substance, believed by alchemists of the Middle Ages to be capable of turning cheap metals into gold, or creating an elixir of life. Symbolically, it represents the final moment of a person's inner transformation, as they finally become truly themselves and reach their full potential. The search for the stone is the quest in book one of the *Harry Potter* series, and it alerts us to the series' alchemical, transformational nature as well as the hero's quest for authenticity — both of which were enduring concerns for **Carl Jung**.

Myths and archetypes

Many stories rely on the idea of the hero's journey, where the main character starts in a position of relative powerlessness and unhappiness, undertakes some form of risky adventure, meets the challenges, and discovers their own power and true self. At one level, this is the story of Harry Potter. However, since we are in the land of mythical people and creatures, we are also in the land of Jung's archetypes. Jung believed that we all have access to a "collective unconscious," a mythopoetic level of mind where archeypes (ancient models) of beings are to be found. Traveling the world, Jung found that the same kinds of figures repeatedly crop up in fairy tales and myths all around the globe, such as the wise old man, the wicked witch and the *puer aeternus* (see page 49) — the Peter Pan type of person who never really grows up. Jung reasoned that these must exist as forms in our minds at birth, deep in the unconscious. When we come across people in real life that coincide with an archetype — such as the trickster — we recognize them and this helps us as we travel through life.

The actual content of a particular archetype, as opposed to its general form, varies from country to country and from one era to another, Jung said. The trickster, for instance, appears in Chinese mythology as the monkey king, in Norse myths as Loki, and in Native American myths as Coyote. We also fill out each archetype depending on our personal experience, so that my idea of the wicked witch would be slightly different to yours, even if we were siblings. In this way the archetypes are a blend of the "mold" we gain from our collective unconscious and our experiences in the external world.

Jungian archetypes are apparent not only in the people we meet, but also as parts of ourselves. The Persona, for example, is the "mask" that we show to others. The Anima is the female element in the male, and the Animus is the male element in the female. The Shadow (see page 112) is the part of ourselves that we like the least — we may even hate this part of ourselves, which we may think of as wicked and despicable.

As with all fairy tales, the characters in the *Harry Potter* books seem to find their match among Jung's archetypes. Dumbledore is a perfect exposition of the archetype *senex*, or Wise Old Man, a bearded figure of great judgment and wisdom, who acts as a mentor to a younger figure. Mrs. Weasley is perhaps the Great Mother, nurturing and creative, while Bellatrix may represent the Terrible Mother, a force of death and destruction (the analyst Melanie Klein would appreciate this split — see page 124). Ron and Hermione may represent the Animus and Anima, while Hagrid is surely the Gentle Giant, an archetype that lives simply and slowly, offering friendship and protection.

Who is Harry?

Harry seems at first to be the Hero, who will set out on a transformational journey, overcoming increasingly difficult challenges until he becomes utterly himself, rather than being made up of other people's ideas of who he is or should be. He certainly suffers from plenty of these throughout the books, as people insist on projecting their various ideas of who he should be onto him, while he tries in vain to resist. The largest of these projections is, of course, the Chosen One, who was born to save the wizarding world. In this role he can be seen as the Divine Child, an archetype that appears extremely vulnerable and weak, but survives against all odds and all the forces ranged against him to flourish and do great things. To Christians, this archetype is exemplified in the narrative of Jesus; to Buddhists, Siddhartha; to Hindus, Krishna. The idea of the Divine Child can be seen across the world's religions and myths. This is not to say that Harry is symbolizing any of these figures, but simply that he is marked out at the beginning as a Divine Child who will save everyone. But, you may ask, is this really possible from the unremittingly dull world of the Dursleys and Privet Drive? Is it possible to emerge from a cupboard under the stairs in suburbia and become a true hero?

> *"Archetypal energies ... can be luminous or dark, angelic or demonic."*
> Donald Kalsched

Archetypes

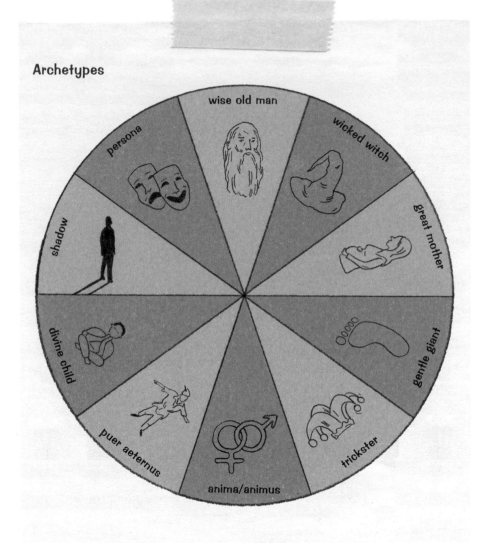

Jung said that we all have access to mythological characters in our minds that we can use to identify types of people in the world, but also to use as alternative personalities following trauma. We recognize the archetypes in fairy tales and fictional magical tales such as the *Harry Potter* books.

Harry doubts this himself and fights against the idea throughout the early part of the series. Jung's idea of transformation was not to become "the best you can be" or some glorious image of ourselves, but to recognize "the law of our own being." By this he meant that we may ultimately be able to recognize what calls us — our vocation — through a total acceptance of ourselves. This sounds simple, perhaps, but the Jungian analysts acknowledge the true difficulty of this task. It involves accepting all the parts of ourselves we don't like (including our Shadow, our Persona, our Animus and Anima) and saying that: yes, this too is me. All of this. Even if it seems embarrassing or risky in some way. If this is Harry's quest, it means that we're heading all the time, throughout the series, toward the point where Harry accepts completely who he is and where his destiny lies. He discovers, finally, that in accepting who he is and the law of his being, he must voluntarily surrender to the evil wizard Voldemort to be killed. Having taken this step, the moment of transformation to full personhood is marked by Dumbledore, who meets Harry in the "other world" to which he is temporarily transported: "You wonderful boy. You brave, brave man."

Archetypal defenses

There is also another level of the story in which Jungian analysts would find meaning. The Jungian analyst **Donald Kalsched** has drawn attention to the role of the archetypes as defensive strategies. When faced with something frightening or extremely hard, we might unconsciously call upon an archetype

and become that "character" to help us get through situations. In extreme cases, where we are so terrified that we "jump out of our skin" (ourselves), we may disappear completely into an archetype as an alternative place to be. Jung said that trauma promotes the formation of "autonomous complexes" (distinct personalities) in the psyche, which, in simple terms, means that during a traumatic event the mind deals with the unbearable reality of what's happening by splitting into different parts. The reason it does this is to compartmentalize the part that has suffered abuse, for example, so that the rest of the person can continue to function. In this way, the child who was abused in the night, for instance, is not the same child who sits down at the breakfast table with their abuser. Life can somehow go on, because it must. This splitting, or *dissociation*, is a protective function of the mind that enables us to keep going when our lives have unendurable experiences. We move into a part of ourselves that "didn't experience that."

The land of dreams

Kalsched (and Jung) suggest that in extreme situations our mind moves to the mythopoetic level, the home of the collective unconscious and dreams, and there it finds archetypes or characters in waiting. Some traumatized children retreat entirely into an inner world of magical creatures and places, which holds an innocent part of themselves in safekeeping and away from the horrors of the external world. Others call upon one, two or more archetypes to inhabit, in the split personalities experienced following dissociation. With this in mind, who is it who is experiencing trauma in the *Harry Potter* books? Who is "splitting"?

In one sense, we can see Harry as the traumatized child, who lives through the terrifying experience of his parents fighting Voldemort to the death, before the evil wizard turns to Harry himself and casts a Killing Curse directly at him. The spell bounces off because Harry's mother Lily refuses to take the offer of being spared, choosing instead to stand in front of her son. Harry's forehead is marked by a splitting symbol — the lightning-bolt scar — but he does not split. The spell is unable to kill him or split him in any way, and this seems to be because love has saved him. His parents did not desert him; he was held and loved for more than a year (he has a secure attachment; see page 100), and this beginning is enough to keep him entire, even though his life is now a difficult one.

However, the same is not true of Voldemort, on whom the Killing Curse rebounds. His physical body is destroyed — his mind is split from his body entirely after this attack on Harry, and for a decade he is said to live in the bodies of others, finally returning to Hogwarts as a face on the back of Professor Quirrel's head. This is emblematic of splitting and dissociation, and it is only later that we realize Voldemort too stems from trauma. His father left his mother when she was pregnant, on learning that she was a witch, and she died shortly after giving birth to him, leaving him to the mercy of an orphanage. He has not felt love and never will; he rages against his fate, vowing to become the greatest sorcerer that ever lived (while Harry repeatedly denies this as a fate) and to cheat death itself (while Harry will ultimately walk voluntarily toward it). In the most vivid depiction of splitting possibly ever written, Rowling has Voldemort split his soul into seven pieces — the horcruxes — which he then hides around the world. All of these must be found and killed if Voldemort is to die finally, and one of these is Harry himself.

Heroes and destroyers

Are Harry and Voldemort the Self and the Shadow of one person, fighting against the effects of trauma in two very different ways? Is Harry proof of the type of survival that is possible when a person has known love from the start, and Voldemort an example of the desperate self who has never known love? These two are united at the very core, says Rowling: they have access to each other's

"Archetypes are considered to be primordial images, spontaneous products of the psyche which do not reflect any physical process, but are reflected in them."
Carl Jung

Carl Jung

"Through the study of these collective transformation processes and through understanding of alchemical symbolism I arrived at the central concept of my psychology: the process of individuation."

> *"From the beginning I had a sense of destiny, as though my life was assigned to me by fate and had to be fulfilled. This gave me an inner security, and though I could never prove it to myself, it proved itself to me. I did not have this certainty, it had me."*
>
> Carl Jung

thoughts, Voldemort cannot touch Harry without feeling intense pain, and their wands actually share the same core — a phoenix feather, representative of coming back to life, of rising from disaster. These two are like one person split by trauma, taking different paths because they have experienced such different pasts. When we experience horror and pain, we may become wise heroes or coldhearted villains, saving the world or vowing to destroy it. Psychotherapy suggests that whether someone has ever truly loved us may make all the difference.

Harry's fictional birthday is 31 July 1980, and the books say that his mother was killed on 31 October 1981, when Harry was 15 months old. In real life, attachment theorists would say that this counts for a great deal, because loving, responsive care during this period is crucial to a baby building a stable core self (see page 123). Neuroscientists such as Allan Schore have not only supported this claim, but shown that the maturation of the brain's limbic and cortical association areas implicated in building secure attachment is completed at the age of … 15 months. (Coincidence? Jung might suggest it is synchronicity.) Schore also notes that separation stress — abandonment — results in protest, despair and detachment. The infant that has never known love or support is unable to feel love or connect to others; they feel utterly alone. The psychoanalyst **Donald Winnicott**

called this a form of "primitive agony" that leads to annihilation of the ego and a feeling of "falling forever," which is countered by creating defenses that are psychotic in nature, such as the archetype of the Destroyer.

If Harry Potter was the boy who lived, Voldemort — Tom Riddle — was surely the boy who died, before even the start of book one, when his body was killed as he attacked Harry. Thereafter, his mind and soul was split into seven pieces and scattered across seven books, all of which seemed to focus on someone else, someone loved, however much Voldemort screamed "Look at me!" But still we turned away. The Divine Child is adored, but the Lost Child is never seen. Perhaps our sense of half-glimpsing the lost child calls us back again and again to these books at least as much as the Hero's journey.

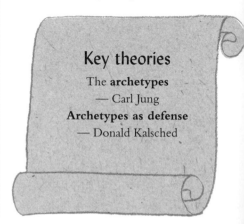

Key theories

The **archetypes**
— Carl Jung
Archetypes as defense
— Donald Kalsched

I wish I hadn't sold that house.

Stuart Hampshire • Janet Landman • Thomas Gilovich • Victoria Medvec
Leon Festinger • Fritz Perls

If you make any choices at all during your lifetime, you're going to regret some of them, which means that the searingly uncomfortable feeling of regret is a given in the human experience. So as the psychologists Thomas Gilovich and Victoria Medvec ask, how can we find a way of dissolving this long-lasting emotion?

There's a large element of judgment involved in regret, much more than would be present in feelings of anger or jealousy, for example. The philosopher Sir **Stuart Hampshire** suggested that this is because regret is cognitively laden to an unusual degree, it requires us to think in a practical way about a decision that we made, rather than simply inspect our feelings. On the other hand it's not only cognitive — it comes with a huge amount of uncomfortable feeling, so it is definitely an emotion, but with a large cognitive input. This is an unusual state of affairs.

So what is regret, exactly? Psychologist **Janet Landman** describes it as an experience of felt-reason or reasoned emotion, which occurs in response to feeling sorry for our misfortunes, limitations, losses, shortcomings or mistakes. As many psychologists have pointed out, a regretted action may be one of commission (where you did something) or omission (where you chose not to do something). It may not even be an *action* you regret; it's entirely possible to regret having *thought* something about a particular person, along with other members of a group, perhaps. However, one thing all regretted decisions have in common is

that you had an element of control; if you were unable to make the decision yourself, the feeling might be disappointment, but it would not be regret.

What if ...?

The way we think, when going over and over something we regret, includes an element of "counterfactual thinking." This is thinking about all the possible alternatives to the path actually taken. It's essentially a kind of "What if ...?" line of questioning that we run internally. (What if I hadn't sold that house then, but a year later, when the market was stronger?) The more easily we can reconstruct events with a better outcome (There are loads of ways I could have handled this better!), the more intense our regret. It's made worse by "closeness" too; if the housing market shot up just a month after you sold your house, it feels worse than if the market hadn't picked up for a couple of years. Yet another intensifying factor is "exception" — if you acted in an exceptional way (perhaps you normally rent for a while when moving to a new district) then you'll kick yourself harder for making that decision.

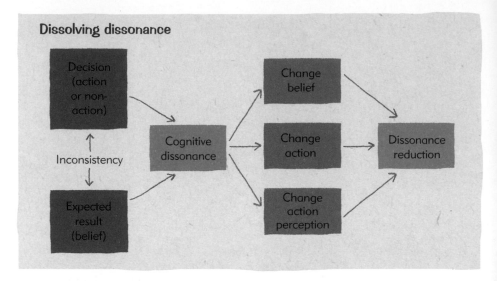

Dissolving dissonance

Decision (action or non-action) → Cognitive dissonance

Inconsistency

Expected result (belief) → Cognitive dissonance

Cognitive dissonance → Change belief → Dissonance reduction

Cognitive dissonance → Change action → Dissonance reduction

Cognitive dissonance → Change action perception → Dissonance reduction

Research also shows that for some reason we regret actions more than inactions over the short term, but over the longer term, it's the failure to act that we regret more. When people have been asked about their biggest regrets in life, they say things like, "I wish I had told my father I loved him before he died," or "I wish I had worked harder at school." **Thomas Gilovich** and **Victoria Medvec** found that it is our regrettable failures to act that stand out and cause greater grief in the end. This may be because if we do something then regret it, we may have a chance to put things right. For instance, if you regret having married your partner, you could get a divorce. But if you said "no'" to someone that you later wished you'd married, that person may have gone on to

marry someone else. The opportunity to act was time specific and allows no amelioration. In addition, because the event was left open-ended (not acted upon) in some way, it was never "closed," so as Bluma Zeigarnik found (see page 75), the brain's "file" on the event stays forever open and the feeling of regret goes on and on.

So how do I get rid of it?

Gilovich and Medvec suggest using something called "dissonance reduction." The psychologist **Leon Festinger** first put the name *cognitive dissonance* to the feeling we get when our beliefs and behaviors conflict with one another — such as carrying on smoking even while knowing it is a major risk to one's health. It also occurs when our

"The ability to be in the present moment is a major component of mental wellness."
Abraham Maslow

> *"I have one aim only: to impart a fraction of the meaning of the word 'now.'"*
> Fritz Perls

thoughts about the world and ourselves clash, so when we make a decision (based on all the information and clear thinking we can muster) and then events turn out badly, the discrepancy between what we expected from the decision and what actually happened results in the uncomfortable feeling of dissonance. This is a state of tension that we're highly motivated to reduce and eliminate, so our brains start trying to do this. Around and around they go, wondering: How can I make this better? How can I get my desires and expectations back in line with what's happened? Can I change the world or put right what I did? Is there any room for change at all?

The first suggestion from Gilovich and Medvec is to put right anything that you can. If you took the wrong course at college, see if you can take it in evening classes now. Then, identify any silver linings, paying special attention to what you've learned from the experience about yourself, other people or the world. If you can identify one or more useful thing that you've learned and are able to say about the experience ("I learned so

Perls' anachronistic thinking

Past (memory) 30% | Present 40% | Future (fantasy) 30%

100% Present

VS.

Perls said that when we make daily decisions based on past experiences or future projections, we are not able to respond with a thorough awareness of the contemporary context and respond specifically to that.

much!") you'll effectively be using dissonance reduction. That's to say, you'll be reducing the tension between the outcome and your intended path of self-growth and self-interest. From this point of view, the decision bought you something good, something worthwhile. Essentially, you're changing the judgment that's in play in this "reasoned emotion," which is all you can do (because you can't change the event). By turning your attention away from the event and toward a different way of thinking about it, you can change one half of the conflict that is creating the feeling of dissonance and so bring the two into line. One of the best ways of doing this is to move to a view of the bigger picture — your whole life — and view the event from there. If, from this view, you can see that you have learned something really worthwhile, the dissonance will dissolve.

I've got to work at it, right?

Not necessarily. Another possible path would be to follow the suggestions of legendary psychotherapist **Fritz Perls**, who, together with his wife, Laura Perls, founded Gestalt therapy. The past doesn't exist, say the Perlses; if you're pondering a memory, you're still in the present thinking back. And your memory won't be accurate anyway, because each time you retrieve and review it, you change it.

"Neurotic thinking is anachronistic thinking," Fritz Perls said. "It is out of place in time." We become depressed thinking about past events that thwarted our desires and then anxious by projecting them into the future, until we're shuffling about in a blur of mounting regret, anxiety, anger and shame. His answer? "Get out of your head and come to your senses!" Literally. Stop thinking, and bring all your attention to your senses. What can you see, hear, smell or touch right now? What's happening to your breathing? By focusing on the here-and-now, your mind will quieten and at the same time open up to the information streaming in from the world around you. "Nothing exists except the 'now'," he says. This is all there is. Stop kidding yourself! (Perls never hesitated to pull punches, such was his enthusiasm for trying to wake us up to our lives.) You need all your attention in the present, so haul it back here if you need to. But bring it here if you possibly can.

Perls famously exhorted people to "be here now" because there isn't anywhere else to go. And if you can grasp this, it works like a magic trick — the entire cognitive dissonance conflict disappears, because it's irrelevant. Gone. Like the disappearing rabbit from a magician's hat. So don't just think about it, he'd say. Do it. Now. (Be. Here.)

Key theories

Dissolving dissonance
— Thomas Gilovich and Victoria Medvec
The **nonexistence** of the **past**
— Fritz Perls

"Present, here-and-now experience constitutes the only reality, whereas memories of the past and expectations about the future are considered fantasies."

Fritz Perls

Should I work for love or money?

Abraham Maslow • Steve Jex • David McClelland • Robert H. Frank

In these generally cash-strapped and economically insecure times, it
would seem logical to pursue job opportunities with greater earnings. However,
since we will spend most of our waking hours at work, we also need to find some
satisfaction in what we do or it will become harder and harder to show up in the
morning, and this may ultimately have a detrimental effect on our well-being. So
which is more important when considering a job offer — the pay or the work
itself? Or is there an easy way to combine both?

Psychologists would suggest that we start
looking at this thorny problem through the
lens of motivational theories — what drives
us to keep going? In 1943, psychologist
Abraham Maslow published a paper
called "A Theory of Human Motivation,"
in which he said that we are motivated by
five sets of needs, which are hierarchical
(see page 54). This means that once the
lowest level of need is satisfied, we are
motivated to pursue fulfillment of the next.

First, he says, we must meet our
physiological needs, for food, water and sex.
Once these are taken care of, we seek to
satisfy our safety needs, making sure we're
protected from physical harm. After this we
look for belonging and acceptance. Then
we want to fulfill our needs for esteem,
such as self-respect, autonomy, status and
recognition. Lastly, when all these other
needs have been met, we strive toward
self-actualization: to reach our full potential
as human beings.

Working with Maslow's thinking, we
can say that money is important in so far
as it helps meet our physiological and
safety needs. This would suggest that we
only need a certain income level — any
amount beyond this would be superfluous
in making us feel good, according to
Maslow. This has been borne out in many
studies, including one in 2010 by economist
Richard Easterlin, which showed happiness
levels across 37 countries do not increase
in tandem with higher incomes.

Making comparisons

On the other hand, our ideas about money
are more complicated than might be
suggested by a reading of Maslow. We are

*"Our needs usually emerge only when more prepotent
needs have been gratified."*
Abraham Maslow

146

especially prone to becoming unsettled by comparison and ideas of unfairness. Occupational psychologist **Steve Jex** found that individuals assess job satisfaction by comparing what they earn with what they believe they *should* earn. He also found that many of our judgments are affected by the people around us, because we look to our coworkers to help us make sense of our environment and even develop attitudes toward it. If our coworkers are positive and satisfied, it seems that we will be too.

Once we start comparing ourselves to everyone else in the company, all sorts of factors come into play. This is because in addition to straightforward salary differentials, there are all those perks to compare, from working in a safer, quieter area to having a parking space or health insurance. Working conditions can be seen to relate to Maslow's third and fourth tiers of need — social and esteem — because they can contribute to a feeling of being valued as part of a team, bringing with it a sense of belonging and respect. On the other hand, where the working environment fails to meet these needs, people can feel isolated, unrecognized for their efforts and undervalued. It seems we need to belong, which includes not only feeling that we are part of a team, but also that we are a valued member of it.

Control and autonomy

The need for respect and social belonging is important to many people, but what about those who have a high need for power and a low need for affiliation? The occupational psychologist **David McClelland** suggested that we only have three motivational needs in the workplace: power, achievement and affiliation. These apply regardless of age, sex, race or culture, he said, but they vary according to our life experiences. Maslow's theory suggests money affects us only to a certain level and then other considerations kick in, but McClelland sees personality playing more of a part. Those who strive toward greater power or achievements may scoop up higher financial rewards on the way, he says, but money is not the key motivator and was never the prime focus. People who strive for greater affiliation enjoy being part of a harmonious group, and their eyes too are not on the money. It seems that McClelland also dismisses the salary on offer as key to decision-making on the job front.

Virtually every study of job satisfaction suggests that autonomy is key. Control over our work and the working day, to some extent, is cited again and again by respondents of surveys as the *sine qua non* of job satisfaction. Maslow places this on his fourth level of need, but it also inches toward the fifth: self-actualization. This is what people mean when they talk about "becoming the best I can be" and it carries within it a sense of what I want, rather than just "what can the company offer me." When this is the focus, comparisons with other people become meaningless and no more than distractions, and this perhaps is the true key to finding the job you love.

> *"If even a tiny fraction of a sufficiently large group of buyers cares about your service, you may be worth a fortune."*
> Robert H Frank

Working conditions can make a place great to work — fun even — but not deeply satisfying. For that we have to look elsewhere.

Flow

The economist **Robert H. Frank** suggests we start with thinking about what we love. What activity absorbs you completely? What kind of thing makes you lose track of time because you're so absorbed in the task that 100 percent of your attention goes into it? This is the experience of "flow" (see page 36). Find this and don't worry about the money on offer, because eventually the money will exceed your wildest dreams. Frank's reasoning goes like this. If you find an activity in which you experience flow, you will naturally and easily become an expert in this type of activity, like Bill Gates, who fell in love with computing at age 13. He had to pay to use the one school computer and, when his money ran out, he hacked into it so that he could carry on. This is not a one-off example of natural dedication leading to success, Frank says; with the onset of globalization and the technological age, becoming an expert is the only sensible way to go.

If, like Gates, you find an activity you love, you'll naturally start spending all the hours you can working away at it, and you'll soon become an expert. The existence of the Internet means that it no longer matters if your expertise is valued locally, because people will find the expert they're looking for (you!) regardless of physical geography. You've become extremely valuable. In this way, by focusing on what you love, you'll gain autonomy, enjoy your working day and reap the highest possible reward. Which means that, in terms of a job search, you need to flip Maslow entirely; reach for self-actualization as the first step and everything else will follow — including a high salary, delicious food (Level 1 needs), a great house (Level 2) and an impressive line of potential partners (Level 3).

Key theories

Theory of Human Motivation
— David McClelland
Hierarchy of Needs
— Abraham Maslow

Understanding

"Human motivation ought to be a good thing. It should help us to find out what we really want so that we can avoid chasing rainbows that are not for us."

David McClelland

Why do I always buy the more expensive option?

Dan Ariely • Leon Festinger • Hilke Plassmann • Bernd Weber

Dan Ariely is the founder of the wonderfully named Center for Advanced Hindsight in Carolina, in the U.S. He suggests that while our behavior is often irrational, it's not random or senseless. There is logic behind our decisions, but it's a kind of "personal logic" based on fact, assumption, biases and our state of mind at the time we're making the decision. Unfortunately, as with most of our behaviors, the bulk of our thinking is biased and unconscious, which is why we're often left wondering: why on earth did I buy that? Is it possible, then, to understand your true motivation for buying and get it under conscious control?

Long before we enter a store or go online to shop, certain assumptions are already in play. The main one, perhaps, is the idea that price signals quality. There are good reasons for believing this: first, it is still true in some cases and, second, the idea that higher price reflects higher value was invariably true at one time. Prior to the Industrial Revolution, the cost of materials and labor dictated the price of products. However, with the onset of mass production, things changed. Those in the new merchant class were in a position to pitch prices according to what they thought we might pay, rather than what the goods had cost to make. This marked the switch from price reflecting objective value (the costs involved in manufacture) to perceived value (what we see things as being worth). It was a slippery slope that we're still sliding down on our credit cards, as we try to convince ourselves that those perfect trainers are well worth the somewhat scary price.

Price expectancy (high)

What happens, then, when we begin shopping? First of all, "price expectancy" comes into play. If we come across a price that feels wrong because it flies in the face of our expectations, our attention is caught. If the price is lower than expected, we feel suspicious. Is there something wrong with it? Is it a fake? Psychologists have also found that we're all risk-averse, which makes us unconsciously biased toward choosing the option perceived to be more safe, which inevitably means "more expensive." Now that low price looks especially worrying.

Next, there's the issue of what a product says about us, or what we think it says. Do I look rich and successful in my Louboutins? Does it mark me out as having a high social status — possibly higher than you? Psychologists are aware of our strong need for comparison all the time, especially in regard to those directly around us. It seems we have a strong desire to look better than everyone else, in every way, all the time. *Social comparison theory*, first formulated by **Leon Festinger** in 1954, states that because there are no objective ways of evaluating ourselves, we do so by comparing ourselves with others — whether on the basis of our abilities, opinions, the homes we live in, our income or the products we buy. "Keeping up with the Joneses" never fails to kick us into action, and how better to signal our superiority in this race than by brandishing a Prada handbag, Mont Blanc pen or Vacheron Constantin watch?

Price expectancy (low)

The flip side of this is the stigma attached to "buying cheap," as though this suddenly positions us as failures in some way. Here it becomes clear that it's not only the image we're projecting to others that's affecting our choices; it's also how those choices make us feel. If buying a cheap version of a product makes you feel like a failure, it may not be a wise choice emotionally even if it's better for your wallet. If you're out shopping with the express purpose of cheering yourself up, fake or cheap probably won't work. Those goods may even act as a daily reminder that you can't afford the "real" ones. It's very easy to allow purchasing habits to affect self-esteem, and researchers have found that low self-esteem is a big factor in determining whether people will buy luxury items they can't afford. When we're doubting ourselves and feeling low, it can act as a way of signaling to ourselves that we are valuable, and worth more, actually, than we feel like

right now. However, with very high price items, this can be both financially treacherous and faulty thinking, because it will not be long before the high from the shopping experience disappears and the guilt reaction sets in.

There are many ways we can shift emotional states, from a depressed low to a feel-good high, for instance. Shopping is one of the most popular and often the most disastrous. It is worth knowing that materialists (who believe that money and

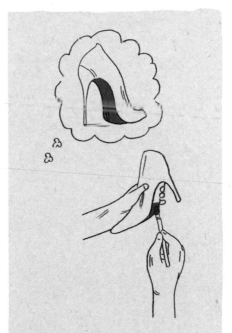

Highly expensive items such as Louboutin shoes (identifiable by their red soles) signal success and wealth, which is why items such as these are often faked by people wanting to send out this message.

possessions are the most important things in life) are the people most likely to overspend, because they believe that the more expensive things they own, the happier they will be. Even given their love of acquiring things, however, something interesting happens around the time of purchase. Studies have shown that they report experiencing greater happiness when anticipating their purchases than after buying them. This suggests that we don't actually have to buy that tempting product to feel good — all we need to do is imagine buying it, perhaps by placing it in a physical or virtual shopping basket, but then leaving it there. As with so many things — from sexual attraction to mobile phones (see page 42) — we get the nice dopamine hit in our brains from the seeking behavior, not from its fulfillment.

Does expensive wine taste better?

In many cases high prices do not reflect higher quality. Nonetheless, our brains can tell us otherwise and there may still be a case for choosing the more expensive option. In one research study by **Hilke Plassmann** and **Bernd Weber**, subjects were asked to sample five different varieties of wine, which they were told were priced at different amounts. In reality, they were only drinking three different types. One wine that cost $5 was offered twice, but was presented as two different wines, costing $5 and $45. Another wine costing $90 was also presented twice, and subjects were told these two "different wines" cost $90 and $10. Not

Cost and enjoyment

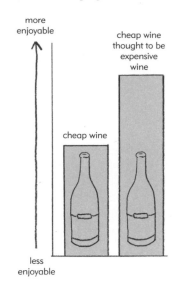

When people drink wine they believe to be expensive, brain scans show they experience it as more enjoyable.

only did people say the wines presented as more expensive tasted better — their brain scans actually showed greater activity in the part of the brain related to pleasure. They actually enjoyed the "more expensive" wines more. The wines were not different, but the increase in price increased the person's objectively measured pleasure. Which means, at some level, it is worth more, doesn't it? Or does it?

Dan Ariely became interested in the part that price and perceived value play in medicine. Is there any benefit in buying more expensively here? Ariely and his research team decided to test this by inviting subjects to test a new drug, Veladone-Rx. The fake "clinical researchers" told subjects that clinical studies showed 92 percent of patients who received the new drug reported significant pain relief within 10 minutes, and that relief continued for eight hours. It cost $2.50 for a single dose, they said. They then exposed each of the subjects to electric shocks, first without pain relief, and then after swallowing Veladone. Most of the respondents reported experiencing less pain with "Veladone," which was actually a placebo. Then the experiment was repeated with identical elements bar one — now each Veladone pill was said to cost 10 cents. In this scenario, fewer than half of the subjects reported decreased pain.

The more expensive the pill, the more effective the placebo. Although expensive versions of aspirin, for example, may not have any additional ingredients, they will work better. Italian neuroscientist Fabrizio Benedetti has demonstrated that this happens because in placebo experiments the brain releases neurotransmitters that use the same pathways as opium and marijuana. The more expensive the placebo, the more natural chemicals are released.

So should I carry on buying expensive stuff?

It seems that high price does not reliably mean higher quality, but it does signal to us that "something special is going on here." Sometimes this is to our advantage — we genuinely experience enhanced medical effect or derive more pleasure from the item. But sometimes it's a distinct disadvantage, particularly when we can't afford it.

Psychologists suggest really noticing context. Is the product next to one that's even more outrageously priced (a "decoy deal") to make the one you like look more reasonable? What mood are you in right now? Are you buying to raise your mood? Or are you with someone you want to impress? Make a slow and conscious decision, as far as you possibly can. This may still involve buying the more expensive product, but for well-thought-out reasons. It's the kind of illogical logic that Dan Ariely might appreciate.

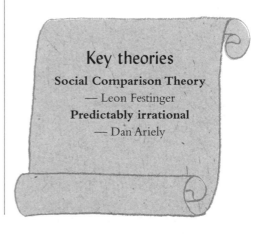

Key theories
Social Comparison Theory
— Leon Festinger
Predictably irrational
— Dan Ariely

What's the point?

Irving Yalom • Emmy van Deurzen • Viktor Frankl • Abraham Maslow • Carl Rogers

This question occurs to most of us every now and then, either in a philosophical way or from a position tinged with despair; the idea that life is meaningless often lies at the heart of depression. There is no easy answer, except for those who adhere to a religious point of view that provides a cosmic overview of the universe and its meaning. However, since the 19th century, the decline in the influence of religion in the Western world has led to a creeping awareness for many that, without religion, life holds no obvious purpose. As the philosopher Jean-Paul Sartre said in 1965: "All existing things are born for no reason, continue through weakness and die by accident ... It is meaningless that we are born; it is meaningless that we die." It is in realizing this very fact, say the existentialist psychotherapists, that we find meaning.

Ancient myths from all around the world suggest that humankind's search for meaning is as old as our existence, and in fact "existence" and "meaning" seem inextricably bound together. As philosophers such as Martin Heidegger have pointed out, we think of a person as being made for a reason, much as we might a pair of scissors, for instance. Something was needed to cut things easily, so scissors were invented. Everything is made for a purpose, so the reasoning goes, which means that human beings must be made for a purpose. Except that we can't find one. Why are we here?

Cosmic or personal?

The existential psychotherapist **Irving Yalom** suggests that finding a meaning is essential to us, because it is through meaning that we acquire values, ideals and goals. It provides us with an entire framework for life and, while the question seems at first to be, "What is the meaning of life?," in reality it is, "What is the meaning of *my* life?" This is the question we're seeking to answer. The first question might be answered with reference to a cosmic framework, such as God, but existentialists explicitly refute this solution. We are here alone, they say, with

"There exists no 'meaning,' no grand design in the universe, no guidelines for living other than those the individual creates."
Irving Yalom

154

> *"We have no predestined fate, and each of us must decide how to live as fully, happily, and meaningfully as possible."*
> Irving Yalom

no prearranged purpose or plan, and we are responsible for what we make of our lives. In this sense the existentialist psychotherapists place huge responsibility on their clients. We have total freedom, they say; and it is through our freely made choices that each of us builds a life with meaning. With no "ultimate law" to fall back on, we must develop our own values, goals and purpose. All this happens, as Yalom notes, against the background of a world where "we can count on nothing besides ourselves to protect us."

If this feels slightly alarming, it's meant to be. With total freedom comes anxiety. How will I know if I am making the right choices? Can I trust myself? The psychotherapist **Emmy van Deurzen** says that anxiety is the shadow side of freedom; they are two sides of the same coin. If I accept a religious path, then I need only follow that, but if everything is wide open — I could do anything! Freedom is not a simple matter of choice; total freedom, including the freedom to choose whether to live or die, is so vast as to be dizzying in its scope. It feels too much, and we may become paralyzed. The philosopher Søren Kierkegaard describes a man standing on a cliff and says that he fears for two reasons: first, he might fall off; second, he might give in to the impulse to jump off. We are staring into the abyss, say the existentialists, and free to choose even between life and death. Everything is up for grabs, and we have only ourselves to rely on.

Existential psychotherapy is the only form of therapy to take its lead from

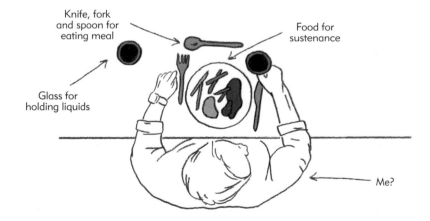

Knife, fork and spoon for eating meal

Food for sustenance

Glass for holding liquids

Me?

We mistakenly think of ourselves as objects, and assume we have been "made" for a purpose, but the truth is, we organically arise, for no reason at all, say the existentialists.

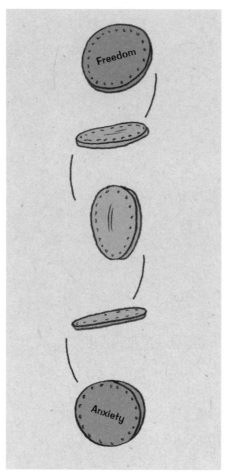

life. But stepping back leads to a kind of death-in-life. If we flee from life and hide away in fear, van Deurzen says, we become disenfranchised, disconnected, unmotivated and despairing. This way lies depression. We need to find the courage to act, rather than falling into an attitude of avoidance or a flight to medication. The skill is in handling anxiety in just the right way — which is to be keyed up enough to come to life, but not so tense that we become dysfunctional.

Always a choice

The psychotherapist **Viktor Frankl** insisted that we always have a choice, even when it seems that all is lost. Frankl qualified as a psychiatrist in the 1920s and went on to work almost exclusively with suicidal patients before being sent to a concentration camp during World War II. Where once he had seen free patients who wanted to die, now he was among imprisoned people who — despite the most horrific conditions it's possible to imagine — struggled to live. In this type of situation, when you have absolutely nothing left, Frankl says, you need to do three things. First, you adopt a cold curiosity about your fate. Then put together strategies to survive. Third, and most important, find a reason to live, for the next few minutes and overarching the rest of your life. This is absolutely essential. It might be a grim sense of humor, a fleeting but amazingly beautiful sunset, or the thought of someone you love. Frankl himself chose to think of his wife, who had also been taken to a concentration camp, as had his parents and brother, and he had no way of knowing

philosophy, viewing itself as the practical arm of existentialism. It sees the freedom of life and its inherent invitation to each of us to find meaning for ourselves as the key to understanding happiness or despair. Anxiety will continually arise and we must choose either to step forward in spite of this feeling or back away from it, opting for a quiet, safe

> *"If there is to be a purpose in life at all, there must be a purpose to suffering and dying, but no man can tell another what this purpose is."*
> Viktor Frankl

whether any of them were alive. His tasks in the camp, detailed in his book *Man's Search for Meaning*, were the stuff of nightmares. If you can find a purpose even for this level of suffering, he said, you can not only survive, but grow as a human being, as many of the people he met managed to do.

Frankl suggests that when we are faced with suffering (or anxiety) we step into the situation knowing that we are always free to choose at least one thing: our attitude toward the situation. In this way we decide what the situation will mean, and this allows us to turn challenges into achievements. He cites the example of a man named Jerry Long, who broke his neck in a diving accident aged 17 and was paralyzed from the neck downward. Long wrote: "I view my life as being abundant with meaning and purpose. The attitude that I adopted on that fateful day has become my personal credo for life. I broke my neck; it didn't break me ... I know that without my suffering, the growth that I have achieved would have been impossible."

The growth that Frankl talks about is the form of personal growth that psychotherapists **Abraham Maslow** and **Carl Rogers** call "self-actualization." This occurs when we stay true to ourselves and choose our own values to live by, rather than mindlessly accepting those handed to us by other people or organizations. Yalom suggests, however, that this is only one part of

finding meaning, and that four other factors may also come into play. Altruism, or serving others in a way that contributes to making the world a better place, will help give our lives purpose. So too does dedication to a cause — whether this is family, country, or a political, educational or scientific movement. Hedonism, or pleasure in the highest sense, such as the awe Frankl experienced at the natural wonder of a sunset while in a concentration camp, helps remind us of the miraculous nature that surrounds us. Lastly, creativity — the skill that allows us not only to improve work, play, relationships and life for others, but also to turn even the most terrible of tragedies into personal triumph — helps give our lives purpose. Happiness cannot be pursued, says Frankl; it can only ensue. But meaning and purpose can — and should — be freely chosen.

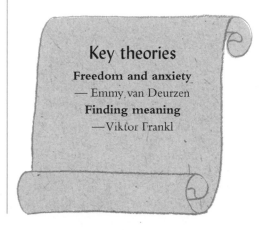

Key theories

Freedom and anxiety
— Emmy van Deurzen
Finding meaning
—Viktor Frankl

How can I improve myself?

Page 160: Why can't I lose weight?

Page 164: I'm scared of moving on in my career — how can I change this?

Page 168: How can I think more creatively?

Page 172: I'm terrified of public speaking.

Page 176: Should I go into Law like my dad wants me to, or join a rock band?

Page 180: How can I cope better with the tough times?

Chapter 5

Why can't I lose weight?

Susie Orbach • Donald Winnicott

This looks like a personal problem that's possibly to do with willpower, but experts from many different fields suggest otherwise. Economists would point out that the global market for weight-loss products is worth hundreds of billions of dollars, so it's not in these firms' commercial interests for us to stop dieting. Are their advertisements part of the reason that you assume you should lose weight and, if you're not, that you're failing in some way? Many of us, it seems, feel bad about being overweight, and doubly so for not being able to diet successfully. But is whipping ourselves into shape really the way to go?

It seems that the more we diet, the more overweight we become. According to the International Food Information Council Foundation, in 2011 more than 75 percent of people in the United States were either trying to lose weight or avoid gaining it. Despite their efforts, nearly 70 percent of Americans were classified as overweight or obese. These figures are indicative of the shame involved in being overweight, and as every psychotherapist would say, shame isn't a helpful motivator for anything.

Bodies as projects

The psychotherapist **Susie Orbach** is the author of *Fat Is a Feminist Issue*, an iconic book on our relationship to food, first published in 1978 and recently updated. The book draws attention to the way in which women's bodies are commodified as objects, and how women themselves are encouraged to adopt this same view. Our bodies are in need of constant improvement, we are told by the food, health, dieting and

beauty industries, and it is up to us to make them smaller, shinier, perkier and more attractive.

In this way women are alienated from their own bodies; they become distrustful of them and their needs, and may even begin to hate them. Appetites, whether emotional (felt in the body) or physiological (such as hunger), come under suspicion. We are told that the body must be controlled. This is a dangerous message. Control operates along a continuum: when we try to control the body too much, things can get out of hand. Recently, as Orbach and others have noted, men have fallen prey to the same objectification, now feeling the need for chiseled abs and perfect pecs in much the same way as women have long aspired to tiny waists and "perfect" breasts (a standard that varies according to fashion, making it impossible to attain and maintain).

In the past there was a wider acceptance that bodies come in all sorts of shapes, as depicted in national art galleries around the world. Nowadays, however, the image of the "ideal" body has narrowed down to one form for each of the sexes: the tall, thin but large-breasted woman and the chiseled, ab-bedecked man. This stereotypical look is now on show everywhere, from New York to Beijing, in defiance of local culture or physical characteristics. In 1995, when television was first introduced to the province of Nadroga in Fiji, the district had experienced only one reported case of an eating disorder. Within three years, 69 percent of adolescent girls reported dieting to lose weight, and 74 percent said they felt "too big or fat."

Modeled on models

Many societies today foster a celebrity culture that involves the constant worship (or denigration) of these "perfect" people. They do a "great" job of looking after themselves, we're told, through eating, exercise, beauty regimes, and you could do this too! The magazines and websites fail to mention cosmetic surgery (except occasionally, to indicate a star's slip from favor) or the fact that many of the images are altered digitally, often against the wishes of the women involved. When actress Kate Winslet appeared long-legged and extremely thin on the cover of GQ

magazine in 2003, she said, "The retouching is excessive … I do not look like that and, more importantly, I don't desire to look like that."

We're swamped by what Orbach refers to as the "mono-imagery" of the perfect male and female types, from their appearance on TV shows and movies, in advertisements on billboards, magazines and websites, and especially on social media. Identifying with these stereotypes, many teenagers attempt to capture the same looks in their profile pictures on social media websites, their strangely posed photographs betraying the unreal nature of the originals. They imitate celebrities and models in the pose, and then compare their selfies with these and with each other. Festinger's social comparison theory (see page 151) says we form an image of ourselves — who we are — by comparing ourselves to others, which includes an element of evaluation. We decide whether we're OK or not by judging ourselves against the norms surrounding us. This leads many teenagers to develop negative images of their own bodies, which may then extend to their whole sense of self.

This phenomenon is not confined to teenagers — in many studies adults too have been shown to judge their bodies against

"People used to know they had problems with their bodies and their eating, and they would come for help. Now it's just taken for granted."
Susie Orbach

Average American
Woman:

5' 4" tall

and weighs

166 lb

Average Model:

5' 10" tall

and weighs only

107 lb

Images of impossibly skinny, tall, white, Western women dominate the representation of beauty in global media, regardless of the physical characteristics of the real women exposed to them. This mono-imagery, or single beauty aesthetic, is unreal; already-thin models are digitally enhanced to portray impossible shapes. In comparing their own real bodies to these images, women invariably feel that they are "letting themselves down" and many begin starving themselves or embarking on painful, expensive surgery to refashion parts of their bodies, such as their nose, eyes, lips or breasts.

media images. A 2006 study by Hesse-Biber, Leavy et al. suggests that adults who access a lot of "thin-ideal media" see thinness as socially desirable. The consequent dissatisfaction with their own bodies leads them to resort to weight-loss regimes and cosmetic surgery in an attempt to measure up to those impossible standards. We are rapidly coming to believe that the digitally enhanced shapes of these "perfect" males and females are not only realistic, but attainable.

Creating bodies

There may also be a deeper level of disturbance about our bodies that can affect our relationship to food. Orbach draws our attention to the "false self" that psychoanalyst **Donald Winnicott** says an ignored, neglected or abused child creates in the hope of winning love. The child assumes that if the parent does not love her, it is her fault in some way — she must be unloveable. Orbach suggests that we do the same thing with our bodies, in response to the type of physical holding, handling and touch that we received during our infancy. All the soothing, the rocking and the swaddling is absorbed at a physical level, giving us a bodily sense of security. Conversely, brusque or inappropriate contact fosters insecurity. If our physical needs were satisfied, we develop a confidence in feeling those needs, expressing them and having them met. We are assured that our physical appetites will be met with pleasure — that they are normal and good. But if these appetites were ignored or reacted to with anger, we imagine that they are shameful and try to reject them. We try to develop a "false body" that is less needy. Since this is not possible, our bodies become a source of constant crisis and insecurity.

There are several ways in which our bodily relationship can be destabilized in different ages, resulting in an unbalanced relationship with food. Normal appetite can become demonized, so food becomes an obsession. The world is waiting with criticism to heap on our heads, saying what's "wrong" with our bodies is our own fault, and we leap into action with self-improvement programs. "We see ourselves as agents, not victims," says Orbach, and apply ourselves to the job of perfecting our own image to match the unreal ones we see around us. We don't see the handcuffs that we place on ourselves and then Houdini-like try to escape them. Since we can't ever achieve our impossible goal, yo-yo dieting is inevitable as we continually oscillate between hope that we'll one day be "thin enough" and despair over our failure to achieve this.

What's the answer?

Orbach suggests that we're asking the wrong thing — it's not a question of how to lose weight, but whether we are willing to learn how to eat and feel comfortable with our bodies. To heal our relationship to food and a normal appetite, we need to rediscover the body's true needs. She offers five "keys" as the way to do this: eat when you are hungry; eat the food your body is hungry for; find out why you eat when you aren't hungry; taste every mouthful; and stop eating the moment you are full. Find ways to listen to your body and accept its needs; focus on yourself, not on the noise of the 24-hour media surrounding us. Otherwise, you will find yourself trapped, eternally, in a fruitless attempt to reach unattainable perfection.

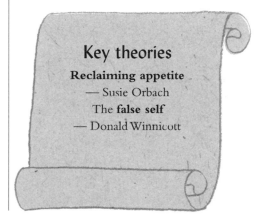

Key theories
Reclaiming appetite
— Susie Orbach
The **false self**
— Donald Winnicott

I'm scared of moving on in my career — how can I change this?

Jaak Panksepp • John Bowlby • Cindy Hazan • Phillip Shaver • Milton Erickson

Neuroscientist Jaak Panksepp would say that whenever we experience a feeling of being afraid to explore, it signals a disruption in one of the brain's primary emotional systems (see page 105), in this case the SEEKING system. This is possibly the most important of the seven systems, because it's what motivates us to get up and go, to look expectantly around ourselves for new opportunities and resources. If it shuts down, we feel depressed and unable to move. We feel stuck, in other words. Finding out what caused the freeze can free you up, or you can cheat and visit an Ericksonian therapist, who will offer to fly under the radar of your unconscious to create instant change.

The shutting down of our SEEKING system may suddenly occur after we suffer a serious loss, such as bereavement or divorce. This is because the intense feeling of separation violates our basic need for attachment and causes another of our primary-process systems, PANIC, to come into play. However, it is also possible for someone's SEEKING system never to have fired at 100 percent, because their basic need for attachment has never been fully met. This is the world of attachment theory (see pages 98–102), whose proponents, such as **John Bowlby**, suggest that we develop secure or insecure personalities based on how our very earliest of needs were responded to. Those who were lucky enough to have their needs responsively met and positively enjoyed saw their parents as a "secure base" from which they could explore. These infants confidently set off to explore the room around them as their parent chatted with a friend, because they felt safe in the adult's presence and could return to their side if need be. On the other hand, babies who felt insecure about their bond to a parent struggled with the wish to explore, being either unwilling to let go, or unable to recognize any need for the adult at all (this is the "duck paddling frantically under water" approach, as the child is panicking even while appearing perfectly calm and detached).

But I'm not a child ...

It seems that our sense of security is lifelong; once gained, we tend to feel secure or insecure throughout our lives, unless we take particular measures to realign our sense of self in the world. This was the main finding of psychologist Mary Main, who demonstrated the continuing nature of our forms of attachment into adulthood. Researchers **Cindy Hazan** and **Phillip Shaver** then looked into how this affects our romantic lives, before wondering about our work lives

Attachments in the workplace

Securely attached
This person will be happy with high levels of job satisfaction. They will get along with colleagues and are likely to be doing quite well and achieving a high income. This person values personal relationships above work, so there may be a picture of a loved one or two on their desk.

Anxious/ambivalent attachment
This person may look preoccupied and unable to concentrate. Their desk may be messy. They are likely to feel misunderstood and underappreciated at work. Due to a fear of rejection, this person will often look worried.

Avoidantly attached
This person doesn't "do" feelings or need people, so you won't find photos or pictures of any kind on their desk. In fact, they are likely to have a very, very neat and tidy desk. They may exude a sense of isolation, such as working away from colleagues and staring intently at their computer screen. This person probably has a high income but doesn't get much job satisfaction, despite working very long hours.

too. We treat love and work as two different realms, they said, but because we're deeply social creatures, won't the way we relate to other people be relevant in workplaces as well as in romances? They also argued that work is functionally similar to Bowlby's idea of exploration; just as babies head off to look at an intriguing blob of raisin on the horizon, as adults we head off into new fields of work to see if the opportunities are real and worth further investigation. We still need adult attachment figures just as we once needed good caregivers in infancy, in order to feel secure enough to go off exploring. Then, they wondered, does our search for work/life (or love) balance reflect the same kind of balance that we earlier experienced in exploration and attachment? In other words, is our attitude to work and our sense of work/life balance actually laid down as children?

Checking It out
Hazan and Shaver looked at the three main styles of attachment and found some interesting correlations between them and our attitude to work. People who were securely attached as children (50 percent of those in the study) reported high levels of work satisfaction in terms of job security, colleagues, income and opportunities for challenge and advancement. They approached their work with confidence, enjoyed it, and were relatively unburdened by fears of failure. However, they valued relationships above their work, and would not allow work to interfere with close relationships. They did not use work to satisfy unmet needs for love.

So far, so good. The second category of attachment, anxious/ambivalent, was found to be associated with far greater levels of anxiety about work and love. This group (19 percent of those in the study) was the most likely to claim that love concerns interfered with work, and Hazan and Shaver suggested this might reflect the old preoccupation with attachment that originally inhibited exploration.

This group of people said they often felt misunderstood and underappreciated, and worried that other people would not be impressed by their performance and reject them. They were easily distracted, had trouble completing projects and tended to "slack off" following praise: a possible indication that their main work motivation was winning admiration from others. They had the lowest average income, even when educational factors were taken into account. Their preoccupation with unmet attachment needs seemed to make concentration on work more difficult, and professional advancement less likely.

The third group, made up of avoidantly attached people (30 percent of those in the study), carried their defining state of detachment with them into work. They were found to be generally dissatisfied with their colleagues, but reported the same levels of job security and learning opportunities as their securely attached counterparts. This group placed more value on work than love and said they would choose work success over romantic success. Like the "avoidant" infant explorers they once were, these people focused on what they were doing rather than the people in their lives, at work or at home.

They acted as if they didn't need people; they tended to use work to avoid having friends or a social life, and didn't enjoy vacations, because they felt anxious when not working. They liked to work alone and, though equaling securely attached people in terms of income, were less satisfied with their jobs.

Reading this, you may have been thinking about your relationship to work, your lifelong sense of freedom (or not) to explore, your current levels of attachment to people around you and your perceived options and position in the workplace. You may have some sense of your attachment style and be wondering about how fixed this is. Fortunately, the relational style we learned as children can be changed through a process known as "earned attachment." Research into the best ways to gain this is still underway, but identifying our attachment styles and understanding them as fully as possible is thought to play a key role in challenging them, along with healing experiences of close, secure and healthy relationships as adults.

Key theories

Attachment theory
— John Bowlby
Attachment and **work**
— Cindy Hazan and
Phillip Shaver

The hypnotic alternative

Earning secure attachment is a lengthy process, so is there is quicker route to job advancement? The psychotherapist **Milton Erickson** recognized the way we absorb thinking patterns during our early years and felt that the only way to change these now unconsciously held patterns was to speak directly to the unconscious. However, the unconscious mind won't accept instructions from the conscious mind (it resists the interference), so he devised a way of speaking that was "artfully vague" and *invited* the unconscious to engage through the use of stories, metaphors, therapeutic binds and contradictions. Technically speaking, he used a five-stage paradigm of trance induction and suggestion (fixation of attention; depotentiating habitual frameworks and belief systems; unconscious search; unconscious processes, and hypnotic response). Non-technically speaking, he flew under the radar and engaged the unconscious.

In recognizing the unconscious as the storehouse of learning, which Erickson saw as naturally healthy and filled with positive intelligence, he found a way to challenge and change someone's self-limiting beliefs with apparently very little effort or time. There are now more than 120 Erickson Institutes around the world treating clients in this innovative way. While these therapists may not be able to deliver a full sense of secure attachment (although Erickson did insist on the necessity to create a "safe base" in the therapy room), they have been found to deliver astonishing rate of change in people's lives for the better. As one participant in a study of Ericksonian therapy said: "Things are just kind of happening; I'm not sure why, but I am more relaxed." And when fear is dissolved, exploration — including your ambitious job search — can finally begin.

"And I want you to choose some time in the past when you were a very, very little girl. And my voice will go with you."
Milton Erickson

How can I think more creatively?

Sigmund Freud • Karl Duncker • Wlodzislaw Duch • Robert Sternberg
Todd Lubart • Ellis Paul Torrance

The great thing about your question is that it assumes, rightly, that everyone is creative, not just the chosen few. Psychologists refer to Big-C and Little-c types of creativity: Big-C turns up in the world looking like the *Mona Lisa* or the Theory of Relativity, while Little-c shows up in the way we choose to dress, change the format of a business report or adapt a recipe. Things we might not notice, in other words, but that are dotted about our daily lives. Does Big-C creativity involve something extra, or can anybody do it?

If you often find yourself avoiding creative tasks by producing a lengthy list of excuses, you may be so busy denying your creativity that you don't notice the originality of those lists. Nor the self-belief with which you confidently deny your abilities, which is one of the key personality traits linked to creativity. Self-belief is crucial because creative thinking often results in ideas that break paradigms and challenge current thinking in a way that others find threatening, whether the idea is a design for a bagless vacuum cleaner or the assertion that the world goes around the sun (which resulted in Galileo being under house arrest for life — its originator, Nicolaus Copernicus, wisely died shortly after publishing the initial theory).

So creativity may be dangerous, which is one reason why you might choose to avoid it. If you were spoken to sternly for the fabulous inventions that you created as a child from the contents of the fridge, garden or shed, you may have learned to keep those interesting ideas to yourself for so long that you've forgotten how to hold onto them when they pop up these days. In addition, memory plays a key role in creativity according to just about everyone, from **Freud** to today's psychologists and neuroscientists, because it seems to be all about thought association. Freud famously encouraged his patients to use "free association," a process that involves tracking thoughts from one to the next and saying

> *"Where there is a creative mind, Reason ... relaxes its watch upon the gates, and the ideas rush in pell-mell, and only then does it look them through and examine them in a mass."*
> Friedrich Schiller, quoted by Sigmund Freud in
> *The Interpretation of Dreams*

Karl Duncker's candle experiment

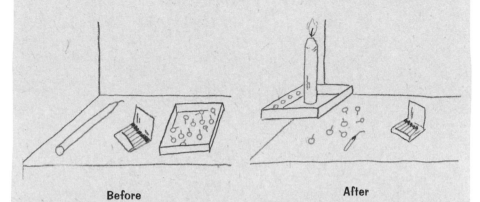

Before　　　　　　　　**After**

The Gestalt theorist **Karl Duncker** came up with an experiment that was designed to show how fluidly or fixedly we think. This is thought to have a bearing on creativity because if we can only think along well-worn paths, nothing new can arise, and novelty is an essential part of being creative. Our solution must also be worthwhile in some way — it's no good coming up with all sorts of new ideas that don't relate to the world or solve a problem in some way. Even musical or literary creativity needs coherence, form and a guiding aim of some sort.

Duncker's experiment was quite simple. He gave each of the subjects a candle, a book of matches and a box of thumbtacks, and asked them to fix the candle to a cork-lined wall in such a way that, when the candle was lit, it would not drip onto the floor below.

The solution is this: empty the tacks from their box, use some of them to attach the box to the wall, then stand the candle in the box and light it. Those of us suffering from "functional fixedness" won't be able to see the thumbtack box as a separate item with many functions, apparently, and may make a fruitless attempt to tack the candle to the wall, despite the inadequate pin-length of the tacks. Anything's worth a try, right? Wrong, apparently. This isn't creative but just plain illogical. We might argue that the "proper" solution doesn't actually result in the candle being fixed to the wall, but the box being fixed to it, which seems like cheating. Didn't he say to fix the candle to the wall? Sadly, even our best arguments will be ignored, despite their own inherent creativity.

> *"The crowd does not maliciously or willfully reject creative notions. Rather, it does not realize, and often does not want to realize, that the proposed idea represents a valid and advanced way of thinking."*
> Robert Sternberg and Todd Lubart

them aloud. By paying attention to all the "involuntary ideas" that came up along the associative path, Freud was able to analyze his patient's woes.

Creative ideas are much the same thing: they arise, says Freud, when people shut down their rational ego and allow more irrational, unconscious connections to be made and to surface. This makes creativity less a form of trying to do something than of "stopping trying," and it is just the kind of less-fixed thinking that would appeal to Duncker (see page 169).

What's the process?

Neurocognitive scientist **Włodzisław Duch** claims that there's a recognizable process that takes place in the brain during creative thinking. It all starts with a preparatory period, during which we consciously introduce (to our brain) all relevant information, which activates corresponding neural circuits in the language area of the brain, and also starts to hook in some other areas that deal with visual, auditory, somatosensory and motor inputs. These brain "subnetworks" are now primed and become highly active, mutually exciting each other (more activity) and forming all sorts of connections while inhibiting others.

Duch claims that for really tricky problems we need to take our time, because we'll need "incubation periods" during which sustained activity of brain circuits means that we make many transient associations; some of these will be short-lived and die fast, while others will be caught and remembered. Duch points out that the incubation stage is what we normally call "imagination" and it seems to be largely an unconscious process. This stage may be followed by days of impasse and even despair, as inhibition takes charge of the process for a while.

Paradoxically, this is a good thing: it means that we're lowering the activity of primed circuits in order to recruit new brain circuits that might help solve the problem. As all this is happening, the most interesting associations make their way to the attention of the "central executive" bit of the brain and become amplified by emotional filters, which leads to further new associations and a bunch of brilliant ideas. Voila!

> *"We all agree that your theory is crazy. The question which divides us is whether it is crazy enough."*
> Niels Bohr

How can I learn to do this better?

Psychologists **Robert Sternberg** and **Todd Lubart** think there are identifiable things we can do to help encourage the imagination-and-filtering process described by Duch. First, they say, we need as much knowledge of the subject area as possible, because we can't move beyond a field of knowledge if we don't know what the original one is. Second, we need to practice certain intellectual skills, including seeing things in many different ways and being able to recognize which ideas are worth pursuing. Third, we need to choose to think in a "legislative" style, meaning that we need to think new and well, not new and poorly. Fourth, we need to cultivate certain traits: we need to be stubborn and full of self-belief, with a willingness to tackle obstacles. Fifth, we need to find a supportive environment, if possible. And, sixth, we need to have an intrinsic desire to do this; we need to be highly motivated.

One of the early researchers into creativity, **Ellis Paul Torrance**, said that this motivation was really the one important thing. He followed the lives of 211 people for more than 22 years in a study of creativity from childhood to adulthood. One of the most important wellsprings of creativity, he said, "seems to be falling in love with something — your dream, your image of the future." Some people have a dream and a clear image of the future, but they're not in love with it — they feel that it is "not really them." So, for a true piece of Big-C creativity, Torrance says that we must search

first for our true identity and then recognize what it is we really love and go for it. In so doing, we'll automatically tick off everything that Sternberg and Lubart suggest without feeling as if we're even making an effort. It will feel like fun.

Of course, says Freud, creativity is linked to play; all children play and give free rein to their imaginations but, as adults, we understand that we need to "grow out of it," so the fantasies that still occur to us, in dreams and daydreams, we keep to ourselves. Our "involuntary thoughts" are liable to meet a most violent resistance, he said, first of all from ourselves, before anybody else. He described the creative person as a "dreamer in broad daylight," indicating the dangerous vulnerability of the creative stance. So perhaps the question is not can you be more creative, but do you dare?

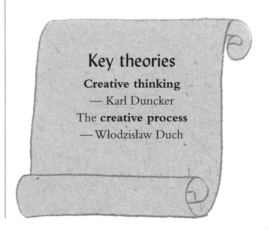

Key theories

Creative thinking
— Karl Duncker
The **creative process**
— Włodzisław Duch

I'm terrified of public speaking.

Alfred Adler

Public speaking strikes fear into the hearts of many of us — so many, in fact, that in 2015 it ranked as the number one fear in the United States and UK, ahead of spiders, deep water, confined spaces, heights, flying and other potential horrors. Many of us simply avoid it, not realizing, perhaps, that while avoidance looks like a great strategy for dealing with anxiety, it actually increases it. So if you want to tackle the fear, rather than avoid it, what helps?

A quick scan of the Internet reveals some of the most common tips for overcoming fear of public speaking. "Know your subject inside out" is a common one, so that if you get lost and stumble, you'll be able to get back on track quickly. (There's a thought destined to increase panic — "I'll never know enough!") Another hot tip is "practice, practice, practice!" implying that public speaking is so hard that you might like to consider bodysurfing instead. "Ignore the audience" is yet another, as though this might magically make you less afraid of the faces in front of you. (Denial is a useful defense in some circumstances, but denying the existence of an entire audience is quite an art.)

In practice, following this advice generally finds us burying deeper into our own thoughts, which tend to be highly negative self-judgments about the many ways we're "totally screwing this up." This can have the effect of making us want to get through the speech or presentation as fast as possible, so we start to talk faster and faster, which in turn makes us take the type of shorter, shallower breaths that act to increase anxiety

still further. Now we're on the way to a full-blown panic attack, while the audience, unaware of all this, might well be sitting there thinking how very interesting the talk is — something that completely passes us by.

Natural inferiority

Anxiety feeds on itself, spiraling ever upward unless we can find a way to interrupt the process or block it when first it appears. The psychoanalyst **Alfred Adler** discovered this at a very early age. He was a frail child, who suffered rickets and nearly died from pneumonia at the age of 5, and this sense of helplessness was to prove critical to his ideas about the lifelong journey of the human self. He said that all children develop feelings of inferiority because at some point they realize their helplessness, and so the struggle toward competence and power defines all our lives. "We all strive to reach a goal by the attainment of which we shall feel strong, superior, and complete," he said, and in so far as we fail to reach this perfectionist image of ourselves, we may develop an "inferiority complex."

Adler also suggested that our minds are both appropriative (taking in everything around us, including what is said about us) and also constructive. We gather up facts and construct meaning from them; life wouldn't make any sense unless we continually knitted it together in this way. However, in many instances we draw conclusions from events in a way that includes some sort of self-judgment, which then becomes part of our view of ourselves. For instance, a child who is continually judged and found wanting assumes that he is defective in some way; each event in which he is shouted at for apparently underachieving confirms his view that his conclusion — such as "I am useless" or "I am stupid" — is correct. This becomes a part of what Adler called our "private intelligence" or personal logic about "who I am." It is full of distortions, but we don't detect this. It feels analytical and thought-through, but in reality it is a set of assumptions, not truths. It is based on a child's immature way of understanding events, an understanding that is self-centered and unable to encompass all the other possible explanations, such as the possibility that the criticizing adult might have been tired, ill or in a bad mood. Once a conclusion has been drawn ("I am useless")

Adler suggests acting as if you are someone brilliant at making speeches, such as Barack Obama. This will allow you to naturally and easily speak fluidly and well.

we take to heart other situations that seems to confirm this, and tell ourselves, "I'm right about that — I *am* useless."

The confirmational bias of the human mind means that from then on we only notice events and reactions of other people in ways that confirm the views we have of ourselves. We're so busy proving ourselves right that we can't change the established view of ourselves. If one of these views is "I can't speak in front of a group of people," it's going to be hard to shift, because it's part of our internal view of ourselves. In a

"Do not be afraid of making mistakes, for there is no other way of learning how to live."
Alfred Adler

strange way, this is how we try to overcome our original feelings of inferiority, according to Adler, because we're proving how "right" we are. This makes us feel superior, even when the thing that we're using to prove this (anxiety in the face of public speaking) seems to run in the opposite direction.

Acting "as if"

Adlerian therapy uses several forms of approach to shift our long-held and faulty view of ourselves. One of these techniques, acting "as if," is a simple way to get started. For any situation in which we'd like to act differently, Adler suggests using those old skills we had as children when we'd dress up as doctors and nurses, or witches and wizards, and role-play so thoroughly that we momentarily lost ourselves in them. Act "as if" you are the person you want to be, he said, because "as people begin to act differently and to feel differently, they become different." Rather than trying to remember a list of things to do perfectly while you're speaking, simply pretend to be someone who speaks easily and calmly — like Barack Obama, perhaps. Let your body adopt his stance and your voice be his, and see what happens. Adler says that if you act as if you are confident, outgoing and assertive — or whatever you feel you lack – you will be.

This is a way to let the body and behavior lead the way, while the mind catches up later and absorbs this new way of being, which gradually becomes habitual. In this way we can use new behavior to form new beliefs about "who I am" and "what I can do."

The benefits of failure

There is an alternative approach that asks us to view the entire situation differently. Mindfulness teacher Gil Fronsdal of the Insight Meditation Center, California, tells a story about a pioneering and highly respected meditation teacher who one day completely "failed" in delivering a talk at a large, prestigious event. She was elderly and very tired, having been caring for a sick partner for many months and then driving overnight to reach the event. While on stage, the same story cropped up several times during her speech. The audience began to get restless and one person stood up to leave. "Wait —" she said, "You're witnessing something very special — you're witnessing one of the senior American Buddhist teachers fail." What was amazing, Fronsdal says, was her relaxed acknowledgment; she did not defend or deny what was happening, but simply accepted it with ease. Her easy relationship with failure demonstrated something more powerful than the content of her speech.

"To be a human being means to feel oneself inferior."
Alfred Adler

> *"Give yourself permission to allow this moment to be exactly as it is, and allow yourself to be exactly as you are."*
> Jon Kabat-Zinn (mindfulness teacher and creator of MBSR)

permission
to fail
GRANTED

What is our response to failure, Fronsdal wonders? He suggested that in meditation we can find out, because in trying to meditate on the breath, for instance, we will find that over and over again we set ourselves to focus on the breath but our minds drift off. What happens when we notice these many small failures? Do we get angry, try harder or give up? Meditation gives us a chance to experience failure and become aware of our response to it. We may notice that we are mindlessly and automatically running thoughts such as "I'm so useless — I'm failing even at this," but now we are in a position to see *that* thought, clearly and perhaps for the first time, unearthing those background assumptions that Adler suggested we make about ourselves. In addition, if we do this during meditation, we are also giving ourselves a safe way to practice failure, so that we begin to see that it's really OK to "fail" and then simply return to what we were doing. We can become comfortable with failure. And from this position, there is nothing to be afraid of.

Key theories

Acting "as if"
— Alfred Adler
Accepting failure
— The mindfulness approach

Should I go into Law like my dad wants me to, or join a rock band?

Karen Horney • Abraham Maslow • Carl Rogers

At the risk of upsetting your dad, it looks as though you may have the entire horde of humanistic psychotherapists on your side, because "self-actualization" (doing your own thing) is seen by them as the ultimate goal of any human life. But this is actually much harder than you might think, because it involves recognizing who you really are underneath all the defenses you've built up over a lifetime. You may feel that your wish stems from an authentic desire, but Karen Horney suggested that we have at least three selves in operation: a real one, an idealized one and a despised one. So which one is holding up the rock-star dream?

The idea of *authenticity* stretches back to ancient times. The Greek philosopher Aristotle proposed that our souls carry within them a potential that must be realized and that this is the true purpose of being alive. Within psychology, this idea was embraced by the humanistic and existential therapists, who were interested not only in working with patients struggling with neuroses, as Freud had done, but also with those who felt well and reasonably happy but wanted to reach for more out of life: to live life to the full.

Self-realization

The person who bridged this particular gap between the psychoanalysts and the humanistic therapists was the German analyst **Karen Horney**. She disagreed with Freud on several points, not least of which was the idea that safety and security figure more highly in directing our good and happy development than sexual desires. Horney also

suggested that we are born with a tendency toward growth, or self-realization, but that social factors (including parents' wishes and cultural norms) interfere with our natural growth, diverting us from a path that we would otherwise have taken.

Each of us is born with an intrinsic self, said Horney, and its initial development depends on how well we "fit" with our parents. If we're naturally very like them, we grow naturally into the people we were born to be; but to the extent that we're different from them, we will be molded into an ill-fitting self. This sense of being molded creates a kind of basic anxiety in us that affects our ability to be spontaneous with other people. It also forces us to hide our true feelings behind false ones and adopt behavior that is deemed more acceptable.

This is where we get really creative. Horney suggested that we develop three types of selves: the real self, the idealized self and the despised self. The real self is initially

The idealized self

The idealized self   The real self   The despised self

a set of genetically prescribed potentialities and dispositions, which will be actualized according to the environment in which we live. The real self includes our temperament, talents and predispositions, and in favourable, nurturing conditions it will grow to its full potential. However, given the less than ideal start that many people experience (because so few parents are in ideal lives themselves), the real self is only a "possible self" that would have developed in that parallel universe. Instead, what most of us develop is an "idealized self," formed from our anxious need to fit in, and in essence it is a defensive stance to carry us through life.

The idealized self

Horney's idealized self (the one we present to others) takes one of three forms: compliance, aggression or detachment. Compliant people form an idea of themselves as loving, caring and forgiving. Aggressive people adopt an idealized self that strives to be powerful, ruthless and triumphant, carrying all before

them. Those who adopt a detached self stand back from others, value freedom and self-sufficiency, and never ask for help.

Since these defensive selves that we form are idealized ("perfectly caring," for example), there is a major downside. We can't live up to them, so we begin to despise ourselves for falling short. The despised self is the one that we feel ourselves to be when we can't reach our own unrealistic standards or demands, and it accounts for our bouts of self-loathing. It is also the source of our tendency to beat ourselves up using the "tyranny of the shoulds." These are the many (possibly everyday) situations when we say to ourselves, "I should do x," and then either comply despite not wanting to, or ignore the "should" and feel strangely guilty and inadequate.

Horney felt that one of the main goals of psychotherapy is to help people let go of their idealized selves — and therefore the despised self too — and accept themselves as they truly are, warts and all. Yet it's surprisingly hard to let go of that attractive

177

idea we have of ourselves. It feels better to be the loving, caring person, or to enjoy the rewards of the powerful boss, or to roam freely around the world unencumbered by compromise. And here's part of your dilemma: when we wish for something, such as becoming a rock star, how do we know whether it stems from our real self or our idealized one? In other words, even if you put aside financial security and your dad's advice in order to follow your own path, how will you know that this wish is truly authentic?

The authentic self

Abraham Maslow picked up the baton from Horney and decided to really get to grips with the authentic self. Both Maslow and Horney thought that it was possible to glimpse the real self occasionally, but while Horney saw this as happening in therapy, Maslow said that it happens when we have a "peak experience." These are "sudden feelings of intense happiness and well-being" that fill us with wonder and awe. We feel totally connected to ourselves and the world, and so in harmony with everything that we experience ecstasy. These experiences may come from small beginnings, says Maslow, such as a mother examining in loving ecstasy her newborn infant, enthralled by every single part of him. It is a "total, non-comparing acceptance of everything." This was an idea that would later arise again as the idea of "flow" in the work of Mihaly Csikszentmihalyi, who also saw this state of total absorption and spontaneous joy as indicating true love with the task at

hand. The search for self-realization and authenticity would also result in the birth of "client-centered" psychotherapy in the hands of **Carl Rogers**, who reasoned that no one other than the client could possibly know what is best for him or her, if the goal is to reach self-actualization.

So perhaps the question to be asked is this: how do you feel when you're playing the guitar? Are you lost in a feeling of oneness with everything that is, and unaware of time and place? Do you have to drag yourself to practice by holding the dream of rock stardom in front of you, or do you reach for your guitar almost without thinking? Maslow would also ask you to check where you stand on his hierarchy of needs (see page 54) before making a career choice, because you need food and safety before you can start reaching for self-actualization, and perhaps your dad has his eye on the lower level of the hierarchy. He's focused on keeping you alive and safe, and anything else is a bonus. You, on the other hand, have your eyes on the greatest prize.

Key theories

The **idealized self**
— Karen Horney
The **client knows best**
— Carl Rogers

"The idealized image is a decided hindrance to growth because it either denies shortcomings or condemns them."

Karen Horney

How can I cope better with the tough times?

Martin Seligman • Viktor Frankl • Boris Cyrulnik • Stephen Joseph • Irving Yalom

The opening line of M. Scott Peck's famous self-help book, *The Road Less Traveled*, hits the nail on the head: "Life is difficult." This idea seems to run counter to the widespread advice to "think positively," which implies a turning away from the bad stuff of life, but researchers into the field of resilience are finding that joining these two ideas together results in transformative growth. Life is difficult, they say, but by facing adversity with optimism and faith in ourselves, we can use it to bring about life-enhancing change.

Resilience is the ability to bounce back after adversity or misfortune. It's the difference between falling into a depression after a year of unemployment or shifting tactics but continuing the search for work. It's the ability to suffer bad news, from the breakup of a relationship or the death of a friend, without becoming overwhelmed by feelings of helplessness. For people who have suffered long periods of continuing trauma or shocking one-off events, such as physical attack, it is the refusal to be defined by that trauma. Resilience is stubborn but not blind or fixed. It is what arises from the depths of despair to put our lives back on track — but, as this happens, it often becomes clear that the track has changed. It's for this reason that many researchers refer to resilience as an ability to adapt and be flexible as much as a set of skills and aptitudes.

Learned helplessness

Martin Seligman, often referred to as the founder of *Positive Psychology*, came to resilience through studying helplessness. In 1975 he carried out an experiment that involved putting three groups of people into rooms from which they could not escape. The first group were subjected to a loud noise that stopped when they pressed a button four times, the second to a loud noise that stopped randomly and independently of their efforts, and the third were not subjected to anything. Later the same day all three groups were exposed to a loud noise, and all were told that they could make it stop simply by pulling a lever. The first and third groups stopped the noise easily, but those in the second group did nothing — they didn't expect their efforts to work, so they had given up trying. This demonstration of "learned helplessness" led to valuable information in the fields of depression and motivation, but one curious finding made little sense at the time. Around a third of people (and animals) who were tested in experiments like this never became helpless. They never gave up. So what was different about them?

> *"Resilience is a sweater knitted from developmental, emotional, and social strands of wool."*
> Boris Cyrulnik

Learning to deal with stress

Stress is something we learn to deal with from the very start of our lives, in small ways that help us realize that we can cope with it. With the help of supportive adults we learn that stress is manageable — we can wait five minutes for a bottle of milk, for example, and turn out to be none the worse for it. On the other hand, if an infant repeatedly screams and screams in hunger but no one arrives for hours, he stops crying (like the adults who stopped trying to turn off the noise). If a child does what he can to get help or to change things and receives no response, he soon learns to stop trying.

Researchers have identified two key factors from childhood that determine resilience in children and adults: the quality and strength of supportive relationships (people responding to our cries), and the key messages we receive about how to view and respond to hardship. If we feel well supported and are taught to view challenges as temporary setbacks that will be overcome, we're likely to feel "naturally" resilient, even though this capacity has in fact been learned. On the other hand, if we grew up with little support or guidance and often felt powerless to control our lives, a form of "learned helplessness" can come home to roost when challenges arise during adulthood.

Learned resilience

The good news is this: learned helplessness was "learned," which means it can be relearned differently. We can increase our resilience at any point in our lives. Seligman suggests that the best way to do this is through "learned optimism." When he began asking the never-helpless subjects of his experiments about their thinking patterns, he found that they thought differently about "the three Ps" — Permanence, Pervasiveness and Personalization. Faced with a setback, they tended to think, "It's temporary, it's just this one situation and there is something I can do about it." Those who gave up and gave in to feeling helpless, on the other hand, were likely to think, "This is going to last forever, it's going to undermine everything I do and there is nothing I can do about it." The first form of thinking gives us a sense of control and power, whereas the second removes all sense of agency. This locus of control is considered to be just as important as the sense of optimism, and it's worth

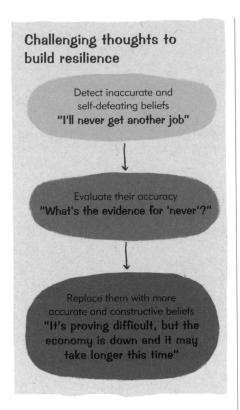

Challenging thoughts to build resilience

Detect inaccurate and self-defeating beliefs
"I'll never get another job"

Evaluate their accuracy
"What's the evidence for 'never'?"

Replace them with more accurate and constructive beliefs
"It's proving difficult, but the economy is down and it may take longer this time"

into resilience. A key part of the program encourages students to detect inaccurate and self-defeating beliefs ("I'll never get another job"), evaluate their accuracy ("What's the evidence for 'never'?"), and replace them with more accurate and constructive beliefs ("It's proving difficult, but the economy is down and it may take longer this time"). Other psychologists suggest also deliberately noticing the "good stuff" — like family, friends, good food, music — to balance out the sense of what's around us. By increasing the field of good stuff, the hard stuff looks less daunting. Search out humor, too, they say, because this reduces tension and also allows a sense of creative "play" to enter our thinking and sit alongside determination. Humor also shrinks the size of the challenge. Both of these strategies increases our sense of control over the situation.

The benefits of adversity

It seems that resilience can be nurtured by understanding that it is not the events themselves that harm or overwhelm us psychologically, but the meaning we give to those events, as the psychotherapist **Viktor Frankl** came to realize after surviving a concentration camp (see page 156). When we don't have the ability to change the situation in the external world, we need to change our internal world; this is the adaptation

noting that this too rests on an internal decision, not external fact. It is within our power to change.

Seligman has devised a course for increasing resilience that teaches people the relevant cognitive-behavioral and problem-solving skills they need to turn learned helplessness

"When an ordeal does come, do we have to succumb to it? And if we fight it, what weapons do we have?"
Boris Cyrulnik

> *"Everything can be taken from a man but one thing: the last of the human freedoms — to choose one's attitude in any given set of circumstances."*
> Viktor Frankl

of resilience. Even if we lose all else, said Frankl, we retain the choice and control over what we think. We can choose to interpret events in quite a different way from the most obvious one, or the one that others attempt to foist on us. We can control our internal world, even in the hardest of times, by deciding on the meaning of events around us.

The psychoanalyst **Boris Cyrulnik** has spent most of his life working with traumatized groups, from genocide survivors in Rwanda to street children in Brazil. He has a lifelong personal interest in trauma and resilience, having survived World War II by going into hiding after his parents were arrested and sent to Auschwitz. He says the resilience of trauma survivors is a paradox, because although the pain is real and never stops, it often provokes "defiance and not groans." There is a fork in the road, Seligman notes, where we need to make existential decisions about our lives — do we give up, like those people trapped in a room with the noise, or do we decide to step forward? Wherever there is extreme change, new doors open to us. If we are paralyzed by depression, we won't be able to open the door to look, but if we can say to ourselves, "I'm going to get through this," we will walk through one of those doors and may find something great — perhaps even the meaning and purpose for our lives that we have so long wished to find.

The potential for trauma to bring about a form of self-actualization has recently become apparent in several fields of research. Psychologist **Stephen Joseph** was astounded to find that 43 percent of survivors of the *Herald of Free Enterprise* ferry disaster (UK, 1987) described their view of life as having "changed for the better." Psychotherapist **Irving Yalom** wonders how many people have lamented, "What a pity I had to wait till now, when my body is riddled with cancer, to know how to live!" Research has shown evidence of "post-traumatic growth" across a wide range of trauma and hardship, including illness, bereavement, sexual assault, terrorist attacks and military combat. In extreme adversity, it seems, our entire priorities and philosophy of life may shift, providing us with incredible clarity and focus, if we can be brave enough to step onto this new path. Resilience is learned but it is also a choice. Perhaps, as Freud said, "From error to error, one discovers the entire truth."

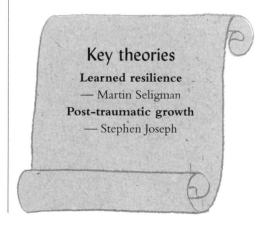

Key theories

Learned resilience
— Martin Seligman
Post-traumatic growth
— Stephen Joseph

Bibliography

Chapter 1

I know I shouldn't — but could you pass that last piece of cake?

Freud, A. (1937) *The Ego and Mechanisms of Defense*. London: Hogarth Press and the Institute of Psycho-analysis

Freud, S. (1960) *The Psychopathology of Everyday Life*. Standard edition (trans. J. Strachey) Vol. 6 (1901). London: Hogarth Press

Freud, S. (1961) *The Ego and the Id and Other Works*. Standard edition (trans. J.Strachey) Vol. 19 (1923–1925). London: Hogarth Press

Freud, S. (1963) *Introductory Lectures on Psycho-Analysis (Parts I and II)*. Standard edition (trans. J. Strachey) Vol. 15 (1915–1916). London: Hogarth Press

Freud, S. (1963) *Introductory Lectures on Psycho-Analysis (Part III)*. Standard edition (trans. J.Strachey) Vol.16 (1916–1917). London: Hogarth Press

Nietzsche, F. (2002 [1886]) *Beyond Good and Evil*. Cambridge: Cambridge University Press

I like hanging out on my own. Is that weird?

Jung, C.G. (1971 [1921]) *Psychological Types*. In *The Collected Works of C.G. Jung*, Vol. 6, 3rd edition (trans. H.G. Baynes). Princeton, NJ: Princeton University Press

Fishman I., Ng, R. and Bellugi, U. (2011) "Do extraverts process social stimuli differently from introverts?," *Cognitive Neuroscience*, vol. 2, no. 2, pp. 67–73

Myers, I.B. and Myers, P.B. (1995) *Gifts Differing*. Mountain View, CA: Jossey-Bass

Myers, D. and Diener, E. (1995) "Who is happy?," *Psychological Science*, vol. 6, no. 1, pp. 10–19

Myers Briggs, I. (2000) *An Introduction to Type: A Guide to Understanding Your Results on the Myers–Briggs Type Indicator*. Oxford: Oxford Psychologists Press

Why do I keep leaving things until the last minute?

Ariely, D. and Wertenbroch, K. (2002) "Procrastination, deadlines and performance: self-control by precommitment," *Psychological Science*, vol. 13, no. 3, pp. 219–224

Burkeman, O. (2013) *The Antidote*. Edinburgh: Canongate Books

Freud, S. (1990) *New Introductory Lectures on Psycho-Analysis*. New York: W.W. Norton & Co.

James, W. (1935 [1886]) Letter to Carl Stumpf (1 Jan 1886), *The Thought and Character of William James*, Vol. 2. Westport, CT: Greenwood

Urban, T. (2013) *Why Procrastinators Procrastinate*. New York: Wait But Why

Am I a caring person or am I a "doormat"?

Horney, K. (1937) *The Neurotic Personality of Our Time*, 2nd edition. New York: W.W. Norton & Co.

Horney, K. (1950) *Neurosis and Human Growth: The Struggle Toward Self-Realization*. New York: W.W. Norton & Co.

Satir, V. (1988) *The New Peoplemaking*. Palo Alto, CA: Science and Behavior Books

Satir, V. (1988) Interview for *Thinking Allowed with Dr. Jeffrey Mishlove*. Oakland, CA: Thinking Allowed Productions

Satir, V., Banmen, J., Gerber, J. and Gomori, M. (1991) *The Satir Model: Family Therapy and Beyond*. Palo Alto, CA: Science and Behavior Books

I was only joking!

Arnold, M.B. (1960) *Emotion and Personality: Vol. 1, Psychological Aspects; Vol. 2, Neurological and Physiological Aspects*. New York: Columbia University Press

Beck, A. Davis, D. and Freeman, A. (2015) *Cognitive Therapy of Personality Disorders*, 3rd edition. New York: Guilford Press

Lazarus, R.S. (1991) "Progress on a cognitive-motivational-relational theory of emotion." *American Psychologist*, vol. 46, no. 8, pp. 819–834

Millon, T. and Davis, R. (1996) *Disorders of Personality: DSM IV and Beyond*, 2nd edition. New York: John Wiley & Sons

Scherer, K.R., Shorr, A. and Johnstone, T. (eds) (2001) *Appraisal Processes in Emotion: Theory, Methods, Research*. Canary, NC: Oxford University Press

Why does it always happen to me?

Damasio, A. (1994) *Descartes' Error: Emotion, Reason, and the Human Brain*. New York: G.P. Putnam's Sons.

Damasio, A.R. (1999) *The Feeling of What Happens: Body and Emotion in the Making of Consciousness*. New York: Harcourt Brace

Seligman, M.E.P. (1991) *Learned Optimism: How to Change Your Mind and Your Life*. New York: Pocket Books

van Deurzen-Smith, E. (1984) "Existential therapy," in W. Dryden (ed.), *Individual Therapy in Britain*. London: Harper & Row.

Watzlawick, P. (1983) *The Situation is Hopeless, But Not Serious (The Pursuit of Unhappiness)*. New York: W.W. Norton & Co.

All work and no play makes Sigmund …

Csíkszentmihályi, M. and Bennett, S. (1971) "An exploratory model of play," *American Anthropologist*, vol. 73, pp. 45–58

Csíkszentmihályi, M. (1975) *Beyond Boredom and Anxiety: Experiencing Flow in Work and Play*. Mountain View, CA: Jossey-Bass

Csíkszentmihályi, M. (1990) *Flow*. New York: Harper & Row

Winnicott, D.W. (1989) *Playing and Reality*. London: Routledge

Winnicott, D. (1990 [1986]) *Home Is Where We Start From*. New York: W.W. Norton & Co.

If I was more selfish, would I have more fun?

Camus, A. (2006 [1956]) *The Fall*. London: Penguin Books

Lerner, M. (1980) *The Belief in a Just World*. New York: Springer Science + Business Media

Lott, T. (2009 [1996]) *The Scent of Dried Roses*. London: Penguin Books

Rowe, D. (2003) *Depression: The Way Out of Your Prison*, 3rd edition. London: Routledge

Rowe, G. and Gale, D. (1991) "Only good people get depressed," *Self and Society*, vol. 19, no. 4, p. 1

Chapter 2

I keep looking at my phone every few minutes …

Broadbent, D.E. (1958) *Perception and Communication*. Oxford: Pergamon

Cherry, E.C. (1953) "Some experiments on the recognition of speech, with one and with two ears," *Journal of the Acoustical Society of America*, vol. 25, no. 5, pp. 975–979

Helmholtz, H. von (1989 [1896]) *Physiological Optics* (2nd German edition, trans. M. Mackeben), in Nakayama, K. and Mackeben, M. (1989) *Vision Research*, vol. 29, no. 11, pp. 1631–1647

Bibliography

Skinner, B.F. (1938) *Behavior of Organisms*. New York: Appleton-Century-Crofts

Skinner, B.F. (1953) *The Possibility of a Science of Human Behavior*. New York: The Free House

Treisman, A.M. (1969) "Strategies and models of selective attention," *Psychological Review* vol. 76, no. 3, pp. 282–299

Treisman, A.M. (2014) *Anne Treisman*. Society for Neuroscience. Accessed online 20 November 2016: https://www.sfn.org/~/media/SfN/Documents/TheHistoryofNeuroscience/Volume%208/AnneTreisman.ashx

Wolfe, J. and Robertson, L. (2012) *From Perception to Consciousness: Searching with Anne Treisman*. Oxford: Oxford University Press

So I'm 50 and wanted a Ferrari. What's wrong with that?

Erikson, E.H. (1963) *Childhood and Society*. New York: W.W. Norton & Co.

Erikson, E.H. (1974) *Dimensions of a New Identity*. New York: W.W. Norton & Co.

Jaques, E. (1965) "Death and middle life crisis," *International Journal of Psychoanalysis*, vol. 46, pp. 502–514

Jensen, G.H. (2009) "Introduction to the Puer/Puella archetype." In S. Porterfield, K. Polette, K. and T. Baumlin (eds), *Perpetual Adolescence*. New York: Suny Press

Yalom, I. (2008) *Staring at the Sun*. Mountain View, CA: Jossey-Bass.

I'm usually so well behaved … what's with the road rage?

Fields, D. (2015) *Why We Snap*. New York: Penguin Random House

Kahneman, D. (2011) *Thinking, Fast and Slow*. London: Penguin

Panksepp, J. (1998) *Affective Neuroscience*. Oxford: Oxford University Press

Panksepp, J. and Biven, L. (2012) *The Archaeology of Mind: Neuroevolutionary Origins of Human Emotions*. New York: W.W. Norton & Co.

Verduin, J. (2013) *Fire and Ashes*. Podcast, 7 July. Redwood, CA: Insight Meditation Center

Why can't I stop giving my time for free?

Adler, A. (1956) *The Individual Psychology of Alfred Adler* (ed. H. Ansbacher and R. Ansbacher). New York: Basic Books

Adler, A. (1997) *Understanding Life*. Oxford: Oneworld Publications (first published as *The Science of Living*, 1927)

Freud, S. (1922) *Beyond the Pleasure Principle* (trans. C.J.M. Hubback). London: International Psycho-Analytical Press

Maslow, A.H. (1970) *Motivation and Personality*. New York: Harper & Row

Maslow, A.H. (1973) *Dominance, Self-esteem, Self-actualization: Germinal Papers of A.H. Maslow*. Monterey, CA: Brooks/Cole

Senay, I., Albarracín, D. and Noguchi, K. (2010) "Motivating goal-directed behavior through introspective self-talk: the role of the interrogative form of simple future tense," *Psychological Science*, vol. 21, no. 4, pp. 499–504

Why do I lie when she says, "Does my bum look big in this?"

Berne, E. (1964) *Games People Play: The Psychology of Human Relationships*. New York: Grove Press

Berne, E. (1973) *What Do You Say After You Say Hello? The Psychology of Human Destiny*. Toronto: Bantam Books

Laing, R.D. (1970) *Knots*. New York: Vintage

Spitz, R.A. (1945) "Hospitalism: An inquiry into the genesis of psychiatric conditions in early childhood," *Psychoanalytic Study of the Child*, vol. 1, pp. 53–74

Spitz, R.A. (1965) *The First Year of Life: A Psychoanalytic Study of Normal and Deviant Development of Object Relations*. New York: International Universities Press.

I'm afraid of flying … what can I do?

American Psychological Association (2000) "Specific phobias," in *Diagnostic and Statistical Manual of Mental Disorders IV-R*

Beck, A.T. (1976) *Cognitive Therapy and the Emotional Disorders*. New York: International Universities Press

Beck, J. (2011) *Cognitive Behavior Therapy*, 2nd edition. New York: Guilford Press

Laker, M. (2012) "Specific phobia: flight," *Activitas Nervosa Superior*, vol. 45, no. 3–4

Tortella-Feliu, M., Botella, C., Llabres, J., et al. (2011) "Virtual reality versus computer-aided exposure treatments for fear of flying," *Behavior Modification*, vol. 35, no. 1, pp. 3–30

Tversky, A. and Kahneman, D. (1973) "Availability: A heuristic for judging frequency and probability," *Cognitive Psychology*, vol. 5, no. 1, pp. 207–233

Last week I drove my car dangerously fast — what was I thinking?

Ceccato, S., Kudielka, B.M. and Schwieren, C. (2015) "Increased risk taking in relation to chronic stress in adults," *Frontiers in Psychology*, vol. 6, p. 2036

Freud, S. (1961) *The Psychopathology of Everyday Life*. Standard edition (trans. J. Strachey) Vol. 31 (1927–1931) *The Future of an Illusion, Civilization and its Discontents, and Other Works*. London: Hogarth Press

Siegel, D. (2013) *Brainstorm*. New York: Penguin

Van Kleef, G., Homan, A., Finkenauer, C. et al. (2011) "Breaking the rules to rise to power," *Social Psychological and Personality Science*, vol. 2, no. 5, pp. 500–507

Zuckerman, M. (1994) *Behavioral Expressions and Biosocial Bases of Sensation Seeking*. Cambridge: Cambridge University Press

Zuckerman, M. (2007) *Sensation Seeking and Risky Behavior*. Washington, DC: American Psychological Association

Zuckerman, M. (2008) "Personality and sensation seeking," in G.J. Boyle, G. Matthews and D.H. Saklofske (eds), *The Sage Handbook of Personality Theory and Assessment. Vol. 1: Personality Theories And Models*, pp. 379–398. London: Sage

Why do I keep watching soap operas every night?

Dunbar, R. (2004) *Grooming, Gossip, and the Evolution of Language*. London: Faber & Faber

Dunbar, R. (2004) "Gossip in evolutionary perspective," *Review of General Psychology*, vol. 8, no. 2, pp. 100–110

Kubey, R. and Csíkszentmihályi, M. (2002) "Television addiction is no mere metaphor," *Scientific American*, vol. 286, no. 2, pp. 74–80

White, E.B. (1982 [1938]) *One Man's Meat*. London: HarperCollins

Zeigarnik, B. (1927) "Das Behalten erledigter und

Bibliography

unerledigter Handlungen" ("On finished and unfinished tasks"), *Psychologische Forschungen,* vol. 9, no. 1

Why do I act like such an idiot in front of my partner's parents?

Daehnert, C. (1998) "The false self as a means of disidentification," *Contemporary Psychoanalysis,* vol. 34, pp. 251–271

Goffman, E. (1956) *The Presentation of Self in Everyday Life.* Edinburgh: University of Edinburgh Social Sciences Research Centre

Miller, A. and Ward, R.N. (1997) *The Drama of the Gifted Child: The Search for the True Self.* New York: Basic Books

Miller, A. (1990) *Banished Knowledge: Facing Childhood Injuries.* New York: Doubleday

Winnicott, D.W. (1965) *The Maturational Processes and the Facilitating Environment.* New York: International Universities Press

Winnicott, D.W. (1987) "Ego distortion in terms of true and false self," in *The Maturational Processes and the Facilitating Environment.* Madison, CT: International Universities Press

Why do I keep buying the same brand all the time?

Kahneman, D. (2011) *Thinking, Fast and Slow.* London: Penguin

MacLean, P.D. (1990) *The Triune Brain in Evolution: Role in Paleocerebral Functions.* New York: Plenum Press

Kahneman, D. and Tversky, A. (eds) (2000) *Choices, Values and Frames.* New York: Cambridge University Press

Tversky, A. and Kahneman, D. (1981) "The framing of decisions and the psychology of choice," *Science,* vol. 211, no. 4481, pp. 453–458

Watson, J. (1913) "Psychology as the behaviorist views it," *Psychological Review,* vol. 20, pp. 158–177

Watson, J.B. (1922) "What cigarettes are you smoking, and why?," *JWT News Bulletin,* pp. 1–17. JWT Archives, Newsletter Collection, 1910–2005, 1916–1922.

Watson, J.B. (1924) *Behaviorism.* New York: W.W. Norton & Co.

Watson, J. (1961) "Psychologists in marketing," *Marketing and Social Research Newsletter of the Psychological Corporation,* 1958. JWT Archives, Dawkins (Colin) Papers, 1776–1986

Watson, J.B. and Rayner, R. (1920) "Conditioned emotional reactions," *Journal of Experimental Psychology,* vol. 3, no. 1, pp. 1–14

Chapter 3

Why can't I find Mr./Mrs. Right?

Fromm, E. (1956) *The Sane Society.* London: Routledge & Kegan Paul

Fromm, E. (1957) *The Art of Loving.* New York: Harper & Row

Fromm, E. (1976) *To Have or To Be?* New York: Harper & Row

May, R. (1969) *Love and Will.* New York: W.W. Norton & Co.

May, R. (1994 [1975]) *The Courage to Create.* New York: W.W. Norton & Co.

May, R. (2009) "Rollo May on existential psychotherapy," *Journal of Humanistic Psychology,* vol. 49, no. 4, pp. 419–434

Plato (2001 [c. 380 BCE]) *Symposium* (trans. S. Benardete) Chicago, IL: University of Chicago Press

Why is the new guy acting so friendly toward me?

Chen, S. and Andersen, S.M. (1999) "Relationships from the past in the present: Significant-other representations and transference in interpersonal life," in M.P. Zanna (ed.), *Advances in Experimental Social Psychology,* Vol. 31, pp. 123–190. San Diego, CA: Academic Press.

Erskine, R. (1999) *The Psychotherapist's Myths, Dreams, and Realities.* Keynote speech from the Second World Congress for Psychotherapy in Vienna, Austria, 4 July

Fenichel, O. (1945) *The Psychoanalytic Theory of Neurosis.* New York: W.W. Norton & Co.

Freud, S. (1912) *The Dynamics of Transference.* Standard edition (trans. J. Strachey), Vol. 12 (1911–1913). London: Hogarth Press

Freud, S. (1955) *Studies on Hysteria.* Standard edition, Vol. 2 (1893–1895)

Nin, A. (1961) *Seduction of the Minotaur.* London: Peter Owen

How do I stop my teenage daughter getting a tattoo?

Blakemore, S., Burnett, S. and Dahl, R.E. (2010) "The role of puberty in the developing adolescent brain," *Human Brain Mapping,* vol. 31, pp. 926–933

Bruer, J.T. (1999) "Neural connections: Some you use, some you lose," *Phi Delta Kappan,* vol. 81, no. 4, pp. 264–277

Crews, F., He, J. and Hodge, C. (2007) "Adolescent cortical development: A critical period of vulnerability for addiction," *Pharmacology Biochemistry and Behavior,* vol. 86, no. 2, pp. 189–199

Huttenlocher, P.R. (1979) "Synaptic density in human frontal cortex — Developmental changes and effects of aging," *Brain Research,* vol. 163, no. 2, pp. 195–205

Jensen, F. and Nutt, A. (2015) *The Teenage Brain: A Neuroscientist's Survival Guide to Raising Adolescents and Young Adults.* New York: HarperCollins

Siegel, D. (2013) *Brainstorm.* New York: Penguin

Steinberg, L. (2008) "A social neuroscience perspective on adolescent risk-taking," *Developmental Review,* vol. 28, no. 1, pp. 78–106

Why is my partner such a loser?

Ainsworth, M. (1985) "Patterns of attachment," *Clinical Psychologist,* vol. 38, pp. 27–29

Bowlby, J. (1944) "Forty-four juvenile thieves: Their characters and home-life," *International Journal of Psychoanalysis,* vol. 25, pp. 107–108

Bowlby, J. (1958) "The nature of the child's tie to his mother," *International Journal of Psychoanalysis,* vol. 39, pp. 350–373

Bowlby, J. (1969) *Attachment and Loss. Vol. 1: Attachment.* New York: Basic Books

Bowlby, J. (1973) *Attachment and Loss. Vol. 2: Separation Anxiety and Anger.* New York: Basic Books

Bowlby, J. (1983) "Attachment and loss: Retrospect and prospect," *American Journal of Orthopsychiatry,* vol. 52, pp. 664–678

Chodorow, N. (1999 [1978]) *The Reproduction of Mothering.* Berkeley and Los Angeles, CA: University of California Press

Main, M. and Solomon, J. (1986) "Discovery of a new, insecure-disorganized/disoriented attachment pattern," in M. Yogman and T.B. Brazelton (eds), *Affective Development in Infancy,* pp. 95–124. Norwood, NJ: Ablex

Main, M. and Weston, D. (1981) "The quality of the

toddler's relationship to mother and to father: Related to conflict behavior and the readiness to establish new relationships," *Child Development*, vol. 52, pp. 932–940.

Wallin, D.J. (2007) *Attachment in Psychotherapy*. New York: Guilford Press

My partner is great — so why am I thinking of having an affair?

Bechara, A., Damasio, H. and Damasio, A.R. (2000) "Emotion, decision making and the orbitofrontal cortex," *Cerebral Cortex*, vol. 10, no. 3, pp. 295–307

Damasio, A. (1999) *The Feeling of What Happens*. New York: Houghton Mifflin Harcourt

Damasio, A. (2012) *Self Comes to Mind*. London: Vintage.

Freud, S. (2001) "An infantile neurosis and other works," in *The Complete Psychological Works of Sigmund Freud*, Vol. 17. London: Vintage.

Kahneman, D. (2011) *Thinking, Fast and Slow*. London: Penguin

Panksepp, J. (1998) *Affective Neuroscience: The Foundations of Human and Animal Emotions*. New York: Oxford University Press

Panksepp, J. (2005) "Affective consciousness: Core emotional feelings in animals and humans," *Consciousness and Cognition*, vol. 14, pp. 30–80

Solms, M. and Turnbull, D. (2002) *The Brain and the Inner World*. London: Karnac Books

How can I stop people unfriending me on social media?

Ellis, A. (2001) *Overcoming Destructive Beliefs, Feelings, and Behaviors: New Directions for Rational Emotive Behavior Therapy*. Amherst, NY: Prometheus Books

Ellis, A. and Harper, R.A. (1975) *A New Guide to Rational Living*. Englewood Cliffs, NJ: Prentice-Hall

Wiener, D.N. (1988) *Albert Ellis: Passionate Skeptic*. Westport, CT: Praeger

Why is my boss always so mean?

Bion, W.R. (1961) *Experiences in Groups*. New York: Basic Books

Girard, R. (1977) *Violence and the Sacred*. Baltimore, MD: Johns Hopkins University Press

Girard, R. (1986) *The Scapegoat* (trans. Y. Freccero). Baltimore, MD: Johns Hopkins University Press

Garard, R. (2001) *I See Satan Fall Like Lightning*. New York: Orbis Books

Jung, C.G. (1947) *On the Nature of the Psyche*. London: Ark Paperbacks

Jung, C.G. (1971 [1921]) *Psychological Types*. In *The Collected Works of C.G. Jung*, Vol. 6, 3rd edition (trans. H.G. Baynes). Princeton, NJ: Princeton University Press

Jung, C.G. (2001 [1933]) *Modern Man in Search of his Soul* (trans. W.S. Dell). Oxon: Routledge

Pines, M. (1985) *Bion and Group Therapy*. London: Routledge & Kegan Paul

My family's a nightmare — shall I cut them off?

Bowen, M. (1966) "The use of family theory in clinical practice," *Comprehensive Psychiatry*, vol. 7, no. 5, pp. 307–462.

Bowen, M. (1985) *Family Therapy in Clinical Practice*. Lanham, MD: Jason Aronson

Bowen, M. (2013) *The Origins of Family Therapy*. Lanham, MD: Jason Aronson

Friedman, E.H. (2007 [1999]) *A Failure of Nerve*. New York: Church Publishing Inc.

Is my partner lying to me?

Ekman, P. (2003) *Emotions Revealed*, 2nd edition. New York: Owl Books

Ekman, P. (2009) *Telling Lies*, 4th edition. New York: W.W. Norton & Co.

Goleman, D. (1988) "Lies can point to mental disorders or signal normal growth," *The New York Times*, 17 May 1988

My boss is so cool …

Fairbairn, W.R.D. (1946) *Object-Relationships and Dynamic Structure in an Object-Relations Theory of the Personality*. New York: Basic Books

Fairbairn, W.R.D. (1952) *Psychoanalytic Studies of the Personality*. London: Routledge & Kegan Paul

Freud, A. (1936) *The Ego and the Mechanisms of Defense*. New York: International Universities Press

Klein, M. (1932) *The Psycho-Analysis of Children*. London: Hogarth Press

Klein, M. (1936) "Love, guilt and reparation," in M. Klein and J. Riviere (eds), *Love, Hate and Reparation*. New York: W.W. Norton & Co.

Klein, M. (1946) *Envy and Gratitude and Other Works*. London: Hogarth Press

Klein, M. (1946) "Notes on some schizoid mechanisms," *International Journal of Psychoanalysis*, vol. 27, pp. 99–110

Chapter 4

Why do I keep saying embarrassing things?

Freud, S. (1960) *The Psychopathology of Everyday Life*. Standard edition (trans. J. Strachey) Vol. 6 (1901). London: Hogarth Press

Freud, S. (1963) *Introductory Lectures on Psycho Analysis (Parts I and II)*. Standard edition (trans. J. Strachey) Vol. 15 (1915, 1916). London: Hogarth Press

Norman, D.A. (1988) *The Design of Everyday Things* (first published as *The Psychology of Everyday Things*). New York: Doubleday

Norman, D.A. (1983) "Design rules based on analyses of human error," *Communications of the ACM*, vol. 26, no. 4, pp. 254–258

Reason, J. (1979) "Actions not as planned," in G. Underwood and R. Stevens (eds), *Aspects of Consciousness, Vol. 1: Psychological Issues*. London: Wiley

Reason, J. (1990) *Human Error*. New York: Cambridge University Press

Reason, J. (2000) "The Freudian slip revisited," *The Psychologist*, vol. 13, no. 12, pp. 610–611

What's the real appeal of Harry Potter?

Jung, C.G. (1953) "Psychology and alchemy," in *The Collected Works of C. G. Jung*, Vol. 12. New York: Pantheon Books

Jung, C.G. (1963) *Memories, Dreams, and Reflections*. New York: Pantheon Books

Jung, C.G. (1968 [1948]) "The phenomenology of the spirit in fairy tales: The Archetypes and the Collective Unconscious," in *The Collected Works of C.G. Jung*, Vol. 9, Part 1. 2nd edition. Princeton, NJ: Princeton University Press.

Jung, C.G. (1970) *Four Archetypes*. Princeton, NJ: Princeton University Press

Kalsched, D. (2013) *Trauma and the Soul: A Psycho-spiritual*

Bibliography

Approach to Human Development and its Interruption. East Sussex: Routledge

Rowling, J.K. (1997) *Harry Potter and the Philosopher's Stone*; (1998) *Harry Potter and the Chamber of Secrets*; (1999) *Harry Potter and the Prisoner of Azkaban*; (2000) *Harry Potter and the Goblet of Fire*; (2003) *Harry Potter and the Order of the Phoenix*; (2005) *Harry Potter and the Half-Blood Prince*; (2007) *Harry Potter and the Deathly Hallows.* London: Bloomsbury

Winnicott, D.W. (1974) "Fear of breakdown," *Psychoanalytic Explorations.* Boston, MA: Harvard University Press

I wish I hadn't sold that house.

Gilovich, T. and Medvec, V.H. "The experience of regret: What, when and why," *Psychological Review*, vol. 102, no. 2, pp. 379–395

Hampshire, S. (1959) *Thought and Action.* New York: Viking Press

Landman, J. (1993) *Regret: The Persistence of the Possible.* Oxford: Oxford University Press

Perls, F.S., Hefferline, R. and Goodman, P. (1951) *Gestalt Therapy: Excitement and Growth in the Human Personality.* New York: The Julian Press

Perls, L. (1991) *Living at the Boundary: Collected Works of Laura Perls* (ed. J. Wysong). Gouldsboro, ME: Gestalt Journal Press

Yontef, G. (1993) *Awareness, Dialogue and Process: Essays on Gestalt Therapy.* New York: Gestalt Journal Press

Yontef, G. (1995) "Gestalt therapy," in A. Gurman and S. Messer (eds), *Essential Psychotherapies.* New York: Guilford Press

Should I work for love or money?

Csíkszentmihályi, M. (1990) *Flow.* New York: Harper & Row

Frank, R.H. (1988) *Passions within Reason the Strategic Role of the Emotions.* New York: W.W. Norton & Co.

Frank, R.H. (2016) "The incalculable value of finding a job you love," *The New York Times,* 22 July

Jex, S. (2002) *Organizational Psychology.* New York: John Wiley

Maslow, A. (1943) "A theory of human motivation," *Psychological Review*, vol. 50, no. 4, pp. 370–396

McClelland, D. (1978) "Managing motivation to expand human freedom," *American Psychologist*, vol. 33, no. 3, pp. 201–210

McClelland, D. (1987) *Human Motivation.* Cambridge: Cambridge University Press

Why do I always buy the more expensive option?

Ariely, D. (2008) *Predictably Irrational.* New York: Harper Collins

Festinger, L. (1954) "A theory of social comparison processes," *Human Relations,* vol. 7, no. 2, pp. 117–140

Plassmann, H. and Weber, B. (2015) "Individual differences in marketing placebo effects," *Journal of Marketing Research*, vol. 52, no. 4, pp. 493–510

Richins, M. (2013) "When wanting is better than having," *Journal of Consumer Research*, vol. 40, pp. 1–18

What's the point?

Frankl, V. (2006 [1946]) *Man's Search for Meaning.* Boston, MA: Beacon Press

Maslow, A. (1968 [1962]) *Toward a Psychology of Being.* New York: Van Nostrand

Rogers, C. (1961) *On Becoming a Person.* Boston, MA:

Houghton Mifflin

Rogers, C. (1980) *A Way of Being.* Boston, MA: Houghton Mifflin

van Deurzen, E. (2001) *Existential Counselling and Psychotherapy in Practice.* London: Sage

van Deurzen, E. (2009) *Everyday Mysteries: Existential Dimensions of Psychotherapy*, 2nd edition. London: Routledge

Yalom, I. (1980) *Existential Psychotherapy.* New York: Basic Books

Yalom, I. (1989) *Love's Executioner.* New York: Basic Books

Yalom, I. (2008) *Staring at the Sun.* Mountain View, CA: Jossey-Bass

Chapter 5

Why can't I lose weight?

Addley, E. (2003) "Faking it," *The Guardian,* 10 January. Accessed online 20 November 2016: https://www.theguardian.com/film/2003/jan/10/pressandpublishing.media

BBC News (2003) "Magazine admits airbrushing Winslet," *BBC News,* 2 January. Accessed online 20 November 2016: http://news.bbc.co.uk/1/hi/entertainment/2643777.stm

Becker, A. (1995) *Body, Self, and Society: The View from Fiji.* Pennsylvania, PA: University of Pennsylvania Press

Becker, A., Burwell, R., Gilman, S. E., et al. (2002) "Eating behaviors and attitudes following prolonged exposure to television among ethnic Fijian adolescent girls," *British Journal of Psychiatry*, vol. 180, no. 6, pp. 509–514

Coleman, S.E. (2007) "Digital photo manipulation: A descriptive analysis of codes of ethics and ethical decisions of photo editors," *Dissertation Archive,* paper 178

Festinger, L. (1954) "A theory of social comparison processes," *Human Relations,* vol. 7, no. 2, pp. 117–140

Hesse-Biber, S., Leavy, P., Quinn, C.E. and Zoino, J. (2006) "The mass marketing of disordered eating and Eating Disorders: The social psychology of women, thinness and culture," *Women's Studies International Forum*, vol. 29, pp. 208–224

Mleyba (2015) "Photos: Great fakes," *The Denver Post,* 4 January. Accessed online 10 November 2016: http://photos.denverpost.com/2015/04/01/great-fakes-famous-doctored-photographs/#37

Matthews, J. (2011) *2011 Food and Health Survey: Consumer Attitudes Toward Food Safety, Nutrition and Health.* Washington DC: International Food Information Council Foundation. Accessed online 20 November 16: http://www.foodinsight.org/2011_Food_Health_Survey_Consumer_Attitudes_Toward_Food_Safety_Nutrition_Health

NHS Choices (2015) "Britain: the fat man of Europe", 29 December. Accessed online 20 November 2016: http://www.nhs.uk/Livewell/loseweight/Pages/statistics-and-causes-of-the-obesity-epidemic-in-the-UK.aspx

Orbach, S. (1978) *Fat is a Feminist Issue.* New York: Paddington Press

Orbach, S. (1980) *Hunger Strike.* New York: W.W. Norton & Co.

Orbach, S. (2002) *On Eating.* London: Penguin

Orbach, S. (2009) *Bodies.* New York: Picador

Bibliography

Williams, Z. (2016) "Susie Orbach: Not all women used to have eating issues. Now everybody does," *The Guardian*, 22 February.

Winnicott, D.W. (2002) *Winnicott on the Child*. Cambridge, MA: Perseus Publishing

I'm scared of moving on in my career — how can I change this?

Bowlby, J. (1969) *Attachment and Loss. Vol. 1: Attachment*. New York: Basic Books

Bowlby, J. (1973) *Attachment and Loss. Vol. 2: Separation Anxiety and Anger*. New York: Basic Books

Erickson, M. and Rosen, S. (1991) *My Voice Will Go With You*. New York: W.W. Norton and Co.

Erickson, M., Rossi, E. and Rossi, S. (1976) *Hypnotic Realities*. New York: Irvington

Hazan, C. and Shaver, P.R. (1990) "Love and work: An attachment-theoretical perspective," *Journal of Personality and Social Psychology*, vol. 59, no. 2, pp. 270–280

Main, M. and Solomon, J.B. (1986) "Discovery of an insecure-disorganized/disoriented attachment pattern," in T. Berry and M. Yogman (eds), *Affective Development in Infancy*. Westport, CT: Ablex Publishing

Panksepp, J. (1998) *Affective Neuroscience*. Oxford: Oxford University Press

How can I think more creatively?

Bohr, N. (1958) quoted in Kaku, M. and Thompson, J (1998) *Beyond Einstein*. Oxford: Oxford University Press

Duch, W. (2007) "Creativity and the brain," in A-G Tan (ed.), *A Handbook of Creativity for Teachers*. Singapore: World Scientific Publishing

Duch, W. (2008) "Intuition, insight, imagination and creativity," *IEEE Computational Intelligence Magazine*, vol. 2, no. 3, pp. 40–52

Duncker, K. (1945) "On problem solving," *Psychological Monographs*, vol. 58, p. 5

Freud, S. (1960 [1901]) *The Psychopathology of Everyday Life*. Standard edition (trans. J. Strachey) Vol. 6 (1901). London: Hogarth Press

Freud, S. (1913) *The Interpretation of Dreams*, 3rd edition (trans. A.A. Brill). New York: Macmillan

Sternberg, R.J. and Lubart, T.I. (1991) "An investment theory of creativity and its development," *Human Development*, vol. 34, no. 1, pp. 1–31

Sternberg, R.J. and Lubart, T.I. (1995) *Defying the Crowd: Cultivating Creativity in a Culture of Conformity*. New York: Free Press

Torrance, E.P. (1983) "The importance of falling in love with something," *Creative Child and Adult Quarterly*, vol. 8, no. 2, 72–78

I'm terrified of public speaking.

Adler, A. (1924) *The Practice and Theory of Individual Psychology*. London: Routledge, Trench, Trubner & Co. Ltd

Adler, A. (1936) "The neurotic's picture of the world," *International Journal of Individual Psychology*, vol. 1, no. 3, pp. 3–13

Ansbacher, H. (1956) *The Individual Psychology of Alfred Adler*. New York: Basic Books

Fronsdal, G. (2015) *Benefits of Failure*. Podcast, 2 November. Redwood City, CA: Insight Meditation Center. Accessed online 20 November 16: http://www.audiodharma.org/talks/audio_player/6113.html

Watts, R., Peluso, P. and Lewis, T. (2005) "Expanding the acting as if technique," *Journal of Individual Psychology*, vol. 61, no. 4, pp. 380–387

Should I go into Law like my dad wants me to, or join a rock band?

Aristotle (1987 [350 BCE]) *De Anima (On the Soul)* (trans. H. Lawson-Tancred). London: Penguin

Horney, K. (1937) *The Neurotic Personality of Our Time*, 2nd edition. New York: W.W. Norton & Co.

Horney, K. (1945) *Our Inner Conflicts*. New York: W.W. Norton & Co.

Horney, K. (1950) *Neurosis and Human Growth: The Struggle Toward Self-Realization*. New York: W.W. Norton & Co.

Maslow, A. (1968 [1962]) *Toward a Psychology of Being*. New York: Van Nostrand

Rogers, C. (1961) *On Becoming a Person*. Boston, MA: Houghton Mifflin

How can I cope better with the tough times?

Abramson, L.Y., Seligman, M.E.P. and Teasdale, J.D. (1978) "Learned helplessness in humans: Critique and reformulation," *Journal of Abnormal Psychology*, vol. 87, no. 1, pp. 49–74

Cyrulnik, B. (2009) *Resilience*. London: Penguin

Dalgleish, T., Joseph, S. and Yule, W. (2000) "The *Herald of Free Enterprise* disaster: Lessons from the first ten years," *Behavior Modification*, vol. 24, pp. 673–699

Frankl, V. (2006 [1946]) *Man's Search for Meaning*. Boston, MA: Beacon Press

Hiroto, D.S. and Seligman, M.E.P. (1975) "Generality of learned helplessness in man," *Journal of Personality and Social Psychology*, vol. 31, pp. 311–327

Joseph, S. (2013) *What Doesn't Kill Us*. London: Piatkus

Joseph, S., Murphy, D. and Regel, S. (2012) "An affective-cognitive processing model for post-traumatic growth," *Clinical Psychology and Psychotherapy*, vol. 19, pp. 316–325

Scott Peck, M. (1978) *The Road Less Traveled*. Delran, NJ: Simon & Schuster

Seligman, M.E.P. (1972) "Learned helplessness," *Annual Review of Medicine*, vol. 23, no. 1, pp. 407–412

Seligman, M.E.P. (1992 [1975]) *Helplessness*. W.H. Freeman

Seligman, M. (2011) *Flourish*. New York: Free Press

Seligman, M.E.P. and Maier, S.F. (1967) "Failure to escape traumatic shock," *Journal of Experimental Psychology*, vol. 74, no. 1, pp. 1–9

Tedeschi, R.G. and Calhoun, L.G. (1995) *Trauma and Transformation: Growing in the Aftermath of Suffering*. London: Sage

Yalom, I. (1989) *Love's Executioner*. New York: Basic Books

Index

Page references for illustrations are in *italics*

acetylcholine 17–18
"acting as if" 174
addiction to television 72–5
Adler, Alfred 55, 172–5
Adolescents *see* teenagers
adversity, benefits of 182–3
affirmations, positive 56–8
affordances 104, 105
aggression 26, 27–9, 50–3
Ainsworth, Mary 98–9
anachronistic thinking *143*, 144
Andersen, Susan 92–3
anger: RAGE circuit 50–2, 53
anxiety 155, 156 *see also* fear
archetypes 134–40
    archetypal defenses 137
    shadow archetype 110–13, 114, 135
"arguing with yourself" 66
Ariely, Dan 20, 152
Aristotle 73–4
Arnold, Magda 27–8
attachment theory 98–102, 164–7
attention span 42–5
authentic self 178
automatic behavior 22 *see also* unconscious behavior
autonomy in the workplace 147–8
availability bias 64

Beck, Aaron *27*, 29, 65–6
behavior
    good vs. bad 37–9
    predictably irrational 150–3
    risk taking 68–71
    sensation seeking 68
    unconscious 19, 20, 22
Benedetti, Fabrizio 153
Berne, Eric 59–62
Bion, Wilfred 113–14
The blamer 24–6
The body, objectification of 160–2
Bowen, Murray 115–18
Bowlby, John 98–102, 164
The brain
    adolescent brain 69–70, 94–7
    creative thinking 170
    and early relationships 99
    habituation 103
    RAGE circuit 50–2, 53
    synaptic pruning 96–7
    triune brain *81*, 82–3
brand loyalty 80–3
Breuer, Josef 10
Briggs, Katherine 15, 16–17
Broadbent, Donald 42, 44
bullying, workplace 110–14
buying, motivation for 150–3

caring behavior 23–6
cars
    driving too fast 68–71
    and midlife crises 46–9
    road rage 50–3
catastrophizing 66
celebrity culture 161–2
"change blindness" 43
Cherry, Colin 42
childhood deprivation 61–2
children
    attachment theory 98–102
    family dynamics 23–4
    play 33–6
    relationship with parents 98, 124–6
    socialization 37–8
choice 141–4, 156–7
closure, theory of 75
codependency 26
"Cocktail Party Effect" 42
cognitive appraisal theory 27–8
Cognitive Behavior Therapy 66
cognitive biases 63–4
cognitive dissonance 142–4
cognitive distortions 65–6
collective unconscious 110–13, 134–5, 137
communication 23–4, 59–62
comparing ourselves with others 150–2
complementary transactions *60*
compliance 26
The computer 24–6
concentration 42–5
conditioned responses 80–3
conflict, external 14
conflict, internal 14, 20–1
coping strategies 24–6
covert attention 45
creative thinking 170
creativity 168–71
crossed transactions *61*
Csikszentmihalyi, Mihaly 36, 72–3
Cyrulnik, Boris 183

Damasio, Antonio 31
The Dark Playground 21–2
Davis, Roger 28–9
death 47, 49, 63–6, 70–1
defense mechanisms 14, 19–20, 26
denial 14, 19
depression 38
desires 10–14
dieting 160–3
differentiation of self 115–18
displacement 14
dissociation 137–8
dissonance, dissolving 142–4
The distractor 24–6
dopamine 17, 45, 68
    and relationships 103–4
    and teenagers 94–5

drama therapy 76–8
driving too fast 68–71
Duch, Wlodzislaw 170
Dunbar, Robin 74–5
Duncker, Karl 169
dysfunctional families 23–4

Eagleton, Terry 71
The Ego 11–12, 13, 20
ego states 59–61
Ekman, Paul 119, *120*, 121–2
Ellis, Albert 107–9
Ellis, Robert Harper 108–9
emotions 31
Erickson, Milton 167
Erikson, Erik 47–9
Erskine, Richard 91–2
existentialist psychotherapy 32, 154–6
external conflict 14
extroverts 15–16, 17

facial expressions and lying *120*, 121–2
failure, benefits of 174–5
Fairbairn, Ronald 124–6
fairy tales 134–5
false and true selves 78, 162–3
families
    games people play 59–62
    relationship with 115–18
    respect for parents 78–9
    rules about selfishness 37–8
family dynamics 23–6
fantasies 15–16
fear 63–6, 172–5
Festinger, Leon 142–3, 150–2, 161
Fields, Douglas 53
flow 148
flying, fear of 63–6
food, relationship with 163
Frank, Robert H. 148
Frankl, Viktor 156–7, 182–3
freedom and anxiety 155
Freud, Anna 10, 14
Freud, Sigmund
    the death drive 70–1
    free association 168–70
    Freudian slips 130–3
    Pleasure Principle 11, 20–1, 54
    psychoanalysis 10–14
    psychosocial development 119
    templates for relationships 91–2, 98
    transference 92–3
    unconscious processing 12, 19, 20, 22, 103
Friedman, Edwin 117
friendliness 91–3
Fromm, Erich 86
Fronsdal, Gil 174–5
fun and selfishness 37–9
functional families 23–4

Index

games people play 59–62
Gestalt psychology 74
Gilovich, Thomas 142–4
Girard, René 113–14
Goffman, Erving 76–8, 79
good vs. bad behavior 37–9
groups 97, 113–14
Guiding Rage Into Power 53

habituation 103
Hampshire, Stuart 141
happiness and play 36
Harry Potter, attraction of 134–40
Hazan, Cindy 164–6
Helmholtz, Hermann von 45
Hierarchy of Needs 54–6, 146–8
hopelessness 31
Horney, Karen 26, 176–8
Huttenlocher, Peter 96–7
hyperrationality 95, 96
hypnosis 10, 167
hysteria 10

The Id 11–12, 20
idealization 123–6
idealized self 177–8
income vs. job satisfaction 146–8
inferiority 55–6, 172–4
instincts, basic 51–2, 53, 70–1
internal conflict 20–1
introverts 15–16, 17–18

Jaques, Elliott 46–7, 49
Jex, Steve 147
Job satisfaction vs. income 146–8
Jung, Carl
    archetypes 134–40
    extroversion and introversion 15–17
    puer aeternus 48, 49
    "self-actualization" 157
    shadow archetype 110–13, 114, 135
"just world" 38–9

Kahneman, Daniel
    cognitive biases 63–4
    fast and slow thinking 52, 103, 106
Kalsched, Donald 137
King, Brian 119
Klein, Melanie 123–4
Kubey, Robert 72–3

Landman, Janet 141
Lazarus, Richard 28
learned helplessness 180–1
learned resilience 180–2
Lerner, Melvin 38–9
life instinct 70–1
life, meaning of 154–7
loneliness 88–9, 90
love 86–90
Lubart, Todd 171
lying 119–22

MacLean, Paul 81, 82–3
magical archetypes 134–40
Main, Mary 99–100, 164
marketing: neuromarketing 82–3
Maslow, Abraham
    Hierarchy of Needs 54–6, 146–8
    "self-actualization" 54, 56, 147, 148, 157, 178
May, Rollo 86, 90
MBTI (Myers–Briggs Type Indicator) 15, 16–17
McClelland, David 147
meaning of life 154–7
meditation 53, 175
Medvec, Victoria 142–4
memory lapses 130–3
men: midlife crises 46–7
metacognition 22
micro expressions 120, 121–2
midlife crises 46–9
Milkman, Katherine 20
Miller, Alice 78–9
Millon, Theodore 28–9
mindfulness 53, 174–5
misinterpretation 108–9
mixed messages see passive aggression
money vs. job satisfaction 146–8
"Monkey Mind" 21–2
moral defense 124–6
motivation 54–6, 146–8, 150–3
multitasking 45
Myers–Briggs Type Indicator 15, 16–17

narcissists 69
needs, hierarchy of 54–6, 146–8
negative thinking 30–2
neuromarketing 82–3
neuropsychology see dopamine; The brain
neuroscience and personality 17–18
neuroses 14
Nietzsche, Friedrich 12
Norman, Donald 130
novelty, seeking 103–5
Nuttin, Joseph 47

Object Relations Theory 123–6
objectification of the body 160–2
optimism 31, 32
Orbach, Susie 160, 161, 162–3
organizations: scapegoating dynamics 111, 113–14
orienting response 72, 73, 75

Panksepp, Jaak
    primary processes 50–2, 53, 105–6, 164
    RAGE circuit 50–2, 53
    SEEKING system 51–2, 105–6, 164

Parent, Adult and Child ego states 59–61
parents see also families
    attachment theory 98–102
    good enough parenting 99, 124
    relationship with 98, 124–6
    respect for 78–9
partners see relationships
passive aggression 27–9
Pavlov's dogs 80
people-pleasing 24–6
Perls, Fritz 143, 144
The persona 110–13
personality types
    Carl Jung 15–16
    Erich Fromm 88–90
    Myers-Briggs Type Indicator 15, 17–18
pessimism 30–2
phones and attention 42–5
The placater 24–6
placebo experiments 152–3
Plato and love 88–90
play 33–6
Pleasure Principle 11, 20–1, 54
positive affirmations 56–8
positive psychology 31, 32
positive thinking 31
power and rule breaking 68–9
predictably irrational behavior 150–3
price expectancy 150–2
primary processes 50–2, 53, 105–6, 164
procrastination 19, 22
productive self 88–90
projection 14, 112–13
The psyche 10–14
psychoanalysis 10–14
psychosocial development 48–9, 119
public speaking, fear of 172–5
puer aeternus 48, 49

questions, asking 56–8, 66

RAGE circuit 50–2, 53
random rewards 44–5
Rational Emotive Behavioral Therapy 107–9
rationality 31
rationalization 19
reaction formation 14
reality and extroversion / introversion 15–16
Reality Principle 11
Reason, James 131
regret 141–4
relationships see also communication; families
    faithfulness in 103–6
    finding the right person 86–90
    games people play 59–62

learning about from TV 73–5
and lying 119–22
perceptions of partners 98–102
and social media 107–9
templates for 91–2, 98
workplace 110–14, 123–6
resilience 180–3
rewards 103–5
risk
real and perceived 63–6
risk behavior 68–71
and teenagers 94–5
road rage 50–3
Rogers, Carl 178
Rowe, Dorothy 37, 38
rule breaking and power 68–9

Satir, Virginia 24–6
scapegoating dynamics 111, 113–14
Schore, Allan 140
SEEKING system 51–2, 105–6, 164
"self-actualization" 54, 56, 147, 148, 157, 176–8
self-belief 56–8
self-control 20
self-esteem 55–6, 58
self-realization 176–7
selfishness 37–9
Seligman, Martin
learned resilience 180–2
positive psychology 31, 32
three dimensions of life 58
sensation seeking behavior 68
The shadow 110–13, 114, 135
Shaver, Phillip 164–6
shopping, motivation for 150–3
Siegel, Daniel 69–70, 94–6
significant-other representation 92–3
Simmons, Carolyn 39

Skinner, B.F. 44–5
soap operas, addiction to 72–5
Social Comparison Theory 150–2, 161
social engagement 97
Social Gossip Theory 74–5
social interactions, learning from 73–5
social media
and attention 44–5
and body image 161–2
and friendship 107–9
socialization 37–8
Solomon, Judith 99–100
Spitz, René 61–2
split personalities 137–8
splitting 123–4
Sternberg, Robert 171
stress 181
suffering 32, 157
super-reasonable strategy 24–6
The Superego 11–12, 14, 20
synaptic pruning 96–7

teenagers
adolescent brain 69–70, 94–6
and body image 161
and tattoos 94–7
and TV soaps 73–5
television, addiction to 72–5
templates for relationships 91–2, 98
thinking
fast and slow 52, 103, 106
negative and positive 30–2
thinking distortions 63–4
Torrance, Ellis Paul 171
Transactional Analysis 59–62
transference 92–3
trauma and resilience 183
Treisman, Anne 42, 45
The triune brain 81, 82–3

true and false selves 78, 162–3
Tversky, Amos 63–4

uncertainty, embracing 39
unconscious behavior 19, 20, 22
unconscious processing 12, 19, 20, 22
Urban, Tim 20, 21–2

van Deurzen, Emmy 32, 155–6
van Kleef, Gerben 68–9
Verduin, Jacques 52, 53
violence: RAGE circuit 50–2, 53
volunteering 54–8

Wallin, David 101–2
Watson, John B. 80–2
weight, losing 160–3
Wertenbroch, Klaus 20
Wilson, Glenn 45
Winnicott, Donald 140
false and true selves 78, 162–3
good enough parenting 99, 124
play 33–5
withdrawal 26
women: midlife crises 47
word slips 130–3
workplace
attachment to 164–7
job satisfaction vs. income 146–8
relationships 110–14, 123–6
working conditions 147

Yalom, Irving
meaning of life 46, 49, 154–5
post-traumatic growth 183

Zeigarnik, Bluma 75
Zuckerman, Marvin 68

Acknowledgments

Huge thanks to the team at Octopus, especially Trevor Davies, Polly Poulter and Ella McLean, for their help in putting this book together. Special thanks also to Dr. Maxine Harrison for her advice, and Gareth Southwell and Grace Helmer for their wonderful illustrations. Lastly, to David, Freya and Lottie, for their wisdom, grace and unfailing good humor, especially during the summer of Freud.